Bible
Scenes

Joshua to Solomon

By Stan J. Beiner

D1569053

Alternatives in Religious Education, Inc.
Denver, Colorado

DEDICATION

To my parents, Betty and Irvin Beiner.
Thanks for handing down to your children
the richness of our tradition, a zest for living
life to its fullest, and the ability to laugh
at ourselves.

© Alternatives in Religious Education, Inc. 1988

Published by:
Alternatives in Religious Education, Inc.
Denver, Colorado

Library of Congress Catalog Card Number 88-70868
ISBN 0-86705-022-5

Printed in the United States of America

CONTENTS

THE BOOK OF 1 SAMUEL

THE BOOK OF II SAMUEL

THE BOOK OF I KINGS

INTRODUCTION

The events that follow the death of Moses and the entry of the Israelites into the Promised Land shaped the character of their religion and brought forth some of the most colorful personalities in history.

The books of Joshua, Judges, I and II Samuel, and I Kings cast light on such problems as the struggles against assimilation, the corruption of power, and the fallibility of even the greatest of heroes. All of these issues have contemporary relevance.

Bible Scenes: Joshua to Solomon consists of a series of short skits covering events from Joshua's conquest of Canaan to the death of King Solomon. The scripts utilize humor to captivate and inform, while emphasizing the basic themes of the biblical text. The skits are appropriate for students in sixth grade through senior high. Older readers will also find themselves smiling.

The skits can be used as a supplement when studying the text to emphasize major points and to provide a change of pace. They are not recommended as a substitute for studying the text.

APPROPRIATE SETTINGS

These skits can be used successfully in a variety of settings. Since the skits are brief synopses of the biblical accounts, it is recommended that the leader and/or students read through the actual text of the Bible before reading a Bible scene.

Bible Scenes can be an enjoyable vehicle for introducing students who have little or no background to the characters and events of the Bible. The skits can be used as the beginning of a lesson on a specific event or moral issue, and again as a summation when concluding a unit. If more time is available, students can also read and analyze the biblical text itself.

For weekend retreats and in camp settings, the skits can be used to explore various characters and events in relation to themes chosen for study.

Whatever the setting, *Bible Scenes* will help students learn and internalize events and personalities in the order they occur in the Bible. These skits will also lead to an appreciation of the sweep and importance of the biblical material.

PRESENTING THE SKITS

In just five or ten minutes, with few if any props and with little or no preparation, a group of students can perform any skit in this book. A variety of options is possible for presenting the skits:

Theatre performance: Any skit can be staged with props and costumes. A series of skits that forms an entire story can be put together for a longer production.

Reader's Theatre: The characters, lined up shoulder to shoulder, can read their parts without any action.

Classroom: Students can be assigned parts to read from their seats.

Plays can be performed by a group of students for other classes, for shut-ins, for groups of parents, or simply for each other. The staging can be as simple or as complicated as desired, depending on the leader, the available time and resources, and the purpose of the production. Staging directions are not included in the text. It is generally best to keep the productions simple and to work out the details among the performers.

As you can see, there are many creative ways to use this book. Many players can read a few parts or a few actors can perform many parts. Words and paragraphs can be deleted and whole sections added as needed. Students can write their own skits based on their experiences with these.

When using *Bible Scenes* as a teaching tool, each reader should have a copy of the book of skits in order to assure a smooth reading.

In the Bible itself, scenes often change abruptly. Such a change of scenes is noted in this book by the use of the symbol * * *. In performing the skits, scene changes can be indicated by merely shifting attention from one center of action to another.

MAPS

Three maps are included in this book and follow this introduction — Canaan Before the Conquest, The Twelve Tribes, and the Kingdom of David and Solomon. Knowledge of geographic locations gives students a concept of why certain events occurred and brings a context to the Bible. Since some of the cities still exist today, the maps also provide a connection between the Israelites of yesterday and today.

CONCLUSION

This collection is intended to serve as a new educational vehicle and to provide a fresh look at a section of the Bible that is often overlooked or inaccessible. And now . . . lights, camera, humor!

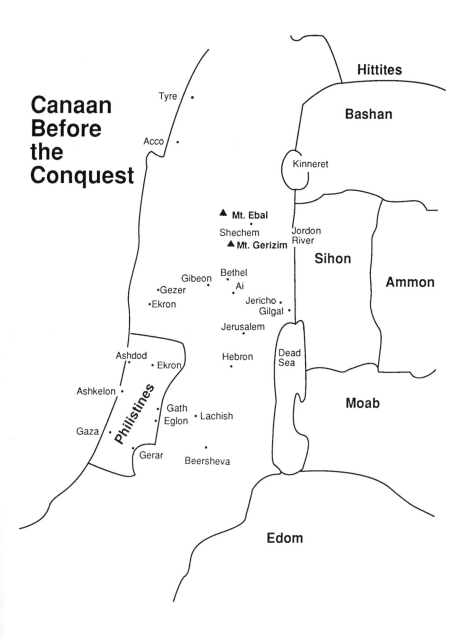

Canaan Before the Conquest

Tyre •

Acco •

Hittites

Bashan

Kinneret

▲ Mt. Ebal
•
Shechem
▲ Mt. Gerizim

Jordon River

Sihon

Gibeon
•
•Gezer
•Ekron

Bethel
• Ai

Ammon

Jericho •
Gilgal •

Jerusalem

Ashdod
•
• Ekron

Hebron
•

Dead Sea

Ashkelon •

Philistines

Gaza •

• Gath
Eglon • Lachish
•

Moab

• Gerar

•
Beersheva

Edom

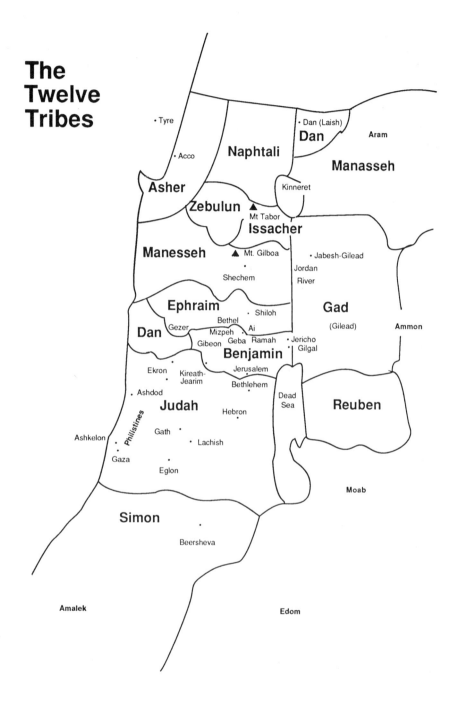

The Twelve Tribes

Tyre

Acco

Asher

Naphtali

Dan (Laish)

Dan

Aram

Manasseh

Kinneret

Zebulun

Mt Tabor

Issacher

Manesseh

Mt. Gilboa

Jabesh-Gilead

Jordan
River

Shechem

Ephraim

Shiloh

Gad

(Gilead)

Ammon

Dan

Bethel

Gezer

Mizpeh

Ai

Gibeon

Geba

Ramah

Jericho

Gilgal

Benjamin

Ekron

Kireath-
Jearim

Jerusalem

Bethlehem

Ashdod

Dead
Sea

Reuben

Judah

Hebron

Philistines

Ashkelon

Gath

Lachish

Gaza

Eglon

Moab

Simon

Beersheva

Amalek

Edom

X

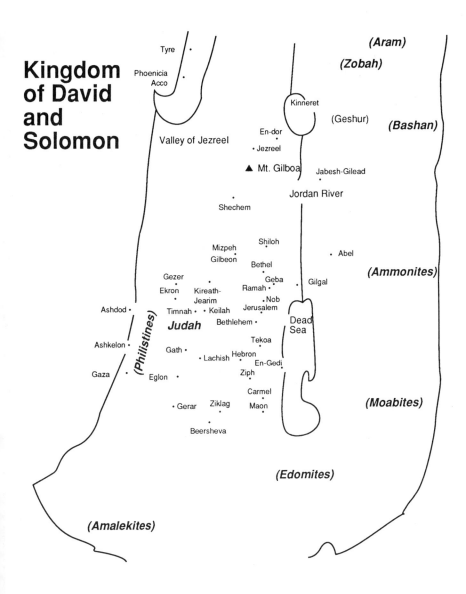

Kingdom
of David
and
Solomon

Tyre

Phoenicia
Acco

(Aram)

(Zobah)

Kinneret

(Geshur)

(Bashan)

En-dor

Valley of Jezreel

• Jezreel

▲ Mt. Gilboa

Jabesh-Gilead

Jordan River

Shechem

Mizpeh

Shiloh

• Abel

Gilbeon

Bethel

Gezer

Geba

Gilgal

Ekron

Kireath-
Jearim

Ramah

(Ammonites)

• Nob

Ashdod •

Timnah •

• Keilah

Jerusalem

Dead
Sea

(Philistines)

Judah

Bethlehem •

Ashkelon •

Tekoa

Gath •

• Lachish

Hebron

En-Gedi

Gaza •

Eglon •

Ziph

Carmel

• Gerar

Ziklag

Maon

(Moabites)

Beersheva

(Edomites)

(Amalekites)

JOSHUA ASSUMES POWER
Joshua 1:1-18

Israelite: Excuse me . . . excuse me. Coming through. I have a very important message for Moses.

Secretary: He's not available.

Israelite: But I just have to see him. I have the latest weather reports from Canaan.

Secretary: How long have you been gone?

Israelite: A few weeks. I zipped across the Jordan to do a bit of spying. Nice country.

Secretary: Well, Moses is no longer with us.

Israelite: Be serious! The guy who took us out of slavery and brought us to the very banks of the Jordan River? The guy who zaps up plagues and chats with the Lord. No longer with us?

Secretary: You've been gone a while and . . . so has Moses.

Israelite: Enough's enough. I demand to see Moses now.

Secretary: Okay. See that mountain over there?

Israelite: Mt. Nebo?

Secretary: He's in it.

Israelite: What do you mean in it? You can't be in a mountain unless you're in the ground, which means . . .

Secretary: Moses will not be taking any more messages. And may I say, you missed a wonderful farewell address. He said some terrific things about following God's laws and he told

1

the whole story of our freedom. My tear ducts were on overload.

Joshua: Shayna, please hold all calls. I am swamped with backlog. How did Moses do it?

Israelite: What's Joshua doing here?

Secretary: He's the new numero uno. I shouldn't say it out loud, but I think we're going to enter the land very soon.

* * *

Narrator: After the death of Moses, the servant of the Lord, God spoke to Joshua son of Nun, Moses' attendant . . .

God: Joshua, you're in charge now. This is the moment for which Israel has prepared these forty years.

Joshua: The football game with the Hittites?

God: Joshua!

Joshua: I'm sorry. I'm just not used to all the pressure yet.

God: Prepare to cross the Jordan. Every spot on which your foot treads I will give to you just as I promised Moses. Your land will extend from the wilderness and the Lebanon to the Great River, the River Euphrates — all the way to the Mediterranean Sea.

Joshua: That's a lot of land for just me.

God: Joshua! For all of Israel.

Joshua: Oh yeah. I knew that.

God: Joshua, I am with you. Be strong and keep the faith. Recite the Book of Teaching day and night and follow it.

Joshua: I have the book right here in my robe pocket.

Narrator: Joshua gave orders to the officials of the people. He told them that in three days time, they would cross the Jordan.

* * *

Reuben: Excuse us, Joshua. We just came by to wish you well.

Joshua: We?

Reuben: Yes, the tribes of Reuben, Gad, and half of Manasseh. We were given permission by Moses to settle on this side of the Jordan. So, good luck. Happy conquering.

Joshua: Shayna, could you come here with the files?

Secretary: Sure. Right here.

Joshua: Could you please refresh everyone's memory?

Secretary: Let's see. Moses says blah, blah . . . etc., etc. Wait a second, I'll get the Ten Commandments file.

Joshua: Not that. The agreement with the two and a half tribes.

Secretary: The camel ate that file, but I distinctly remember Moses promised Reuben, Gad, and half of Manasseh that they could settle east of the Jordan providing they help with the conquering of the land.

Joshua: Now, we don't want to forget binding agreements with Moses and the Lord who split the sea and sent the plagues, do we?

Reuben: It's coming back to us now.

Gad: Oh right. The agreement. Silly us. What should we do?

Joshua: Leave your wives and children in the territory assigned to you. Your fighting men shall go across armed in the company of your kinsmen. You shall assist them until the land is in their possession. Then you may return to the territory east of the Jordan that Moses assigned to you.

Reuben: We will follow your command just as we obeyed Moses.

Narrator: And so the Israelites prepared to enter the land of Canaan with Joshua, the new leader of the people.

SPIES IN JERICHO
Joshua 2:1-24

Spy 1: Are you sure no one suspects us?

Spy 2: Trust me. How are they going to tell that we are Israelites? We blend in with the crowd perfectly. We look like a couple of shepherds in Jericho for a good time.

Spy 1: What exactly does Joshua want us to look for?

Spy 2: He probably just wants us to see if they have any secret weapons.

Spy 1: They don't need secret weapons. They have the biggest wall I've ever seen.

Spy 2: We've been in the desert for forty years. It's the only wall you've ever seen.

Spy 1: Let's take a quick look and get out of here. I don't want to get caught. You know what they do to spies?

Spy 2: Quit worrying. We look like Canaanites.

Newsboy: Extra! Extra! Read all about it. Israelite spies reported in the city. King has ordered an All Points Bulletin. They are easy to spot because they look different and have funny accents.

Spy 1: We blend in! Just a couple of shepherds looking for a good time! We better hide. Hurry, into this . . . tavern.

Rahab: Can I help you?

Spy 1: Two desert fizzes. (whispers) Try not to look conspicuous.

Rahab: What kind of drink is that, country boy? I've never heard of it.

Spy 2: Gin, seltzer, and goat milk.

Spy 1: What's a nice girl like you doing in a place like this?

Rahab: A girl has to make a living! Say, you must be the Israelite spies that everyone is looking for.

Spy 1: Who us? No. We're down here for some fishing.

Rahab: I don't think so.

Spy 2: How come?

Rahab: You have fringes on your clothes you have heavy accents, and you just paid me in shekels.

Spy 2: You call that proof?

Rahab: I'm not going to turn you in. Go upstairs on the roof and take a nap. You can relax on the flax.

Spy 1: Flax? After forty years in the desert, we were sort of hoping for a . . . waterbed.

Rahab: Upstairs, quickly. The king is bound to send his men here looking for you.

Spy 2: How do you know that?

Rahab: Because it says so in chapter 2, verse 3.

Guard 1: Knock knock. Any spies in there?

Rahab: Yeah! I have a whole room full.

Guard 2: We have orders to search your place, Rahab. People say that the Israelites are here.

Rahab: Israelites? What Israelites?

Guard 1: We have eyewitnesses who say that two men in

funny clothes and carrying a lot of souvenirs entered this place.

Rahab: Oh, *those* Israelites. They got out of Jericho at sundown, just before the gates closed. They couldn't have gotten far. I'll bet you can catch them if you hurry.

Spy 1: Is it safe to come down, yet?

Rahab: You're going to have to stay on the roof tonight. The guards are everywhere.

Spy 2: Thanks for everything, Rahab. I wish there was a way to repay you.

Rahab: I'm glad you mentioned pay, because I'm not in the habit of working for nothing. I know the Israelites are going to attack Jericho and take over the land.

Spy 1: We're going to try. But you have such a big wall.

Rahab: On our side are a bunch of silly wooden idols and a king whose idea of giving orders is going to the Chinese takeout. On your side is God, the One who dried up the Sea of Reeds . . . and a bunch of dynamite trumpet players. So who do you think is going to win?

Spy 2: What about your armies?

Rahab: They're shaking in their sandals. Now, I've been helpful to you. In return I want you to promise me that my family will be safe when Israel conquers Jericho. Provide me with a reliable sign so I can trust you to keep your word.

Spy 1: A reliable sign? How about this rabbit's foot that belonged to my grandfather?

Rahab: I don't think a rabbit's foot is a reliable sign.

Spy 2: All right, we give our personal pledge to you on our lives.

Rahab: That's what I call a good sign.

Spy 1: Our lives? You pledged our lives!

Spy 2: Rahab has saved us. We will save her. Rahab, when the battle begins, hang a crimson cord from your window and gather your family inside your house. If you forget, we are released from our pledge.

Narrator: And Rahab let the men down by a rope through the window, for her dwelling was at the outer side of the city wall and she lived in the actual wall. And the two men reported to Joshua that Jericho was . . . scared bonkers.

CROSSING THE JORDAN

Joshua 3:1-4:24

Narrator: Joshua and all the Israelites set out from Shittim and marched to the Jordan.

Director: I want everything in place. I don't want to miss a single shot.

Assistant: What's the big deal?

Director: The big deal is that Joshua is going to perform his first miracle. Instinct tells me that something big is about to happen. Oh, I can feel it in my bones.

Assistant: The entire nation is lined up by the Jordan and the priests are at the edge of the water with the Holy Ark. Even a child could tell that something big is about to happen.

Director: Joshua is about to speak. Get the cameras on Joshua.

Joshua: Come close and hear the words of the Lord your God. You shall know that a living God is among you, a God who will dispossess for you the Canaanites, Hittites, Hivites, Perizzites, Girgashites, Amorites, and Jebusites.

Director: Quick . . . voice over to live commentary.

Yehuda: This is Yehuda Yorad with Barbara Mayim. We are witnessing Joshua's first real press conference. He looks very confident. That's quite a hit list he has. Barbara, your comments?

Barbara: I have to agree. Joshua looks very good. He is wearing a lovely outfit that just commands respect. And I haven't seen the Ark look spiffier since our battle with the Amorites.

Joshua: When the feet of the priests bearing the Ark of the

9

Lord come to rest in the waters of the Jordan, the water from upstream will be cut off and stand in a single heap.

Director: Holy Moses. He's going for the splitting of the waters miracle. Here comes an academy award for sure. DeMille gets the Red Sea and I get the Jordan River. Cameras ready and . . . action!

Priest 1: How long do we have to stand in the middle of the Jordan River holding the Ark of the Covenant?

Priest 2: Until the entire nation has crossed.

Priest 3: We have been standing in the middle of the Jordan for hours holding up the Ark. Anyone have something for back pain?

Priest 2: Kvetch, kvetch, kvetch. We are making history.

Priest 1: Hey, do you see what I see?

Priest 3: The end of the line! See that couple holding hands. They're the last ones.

Priest 1: Why are they stopping? They're making goo-goo eyes. Hey, you two — save that for the other side. We've got serious back problems.

Priest 3: Here comes Joshua.

Joshua: Twelve men . . . one from each of the tribes . . . will take a stone from the middle of the river and carry it to the other side where it shall be set with all the other stones as a memorial for this day.

Priest 1: I hope this ceremony can be kept to a minimum.

Narrator: And when all the people finished crossing, the priests with the Ark of the Covenant advanced to the head of the people.

Priest 3: Coming through. 'Scuse us. Move aside. Coming through.

Priest 2: Let it down easy . . . easy.

Priests: Ahhhhhhhh!

Director: That's a wrap. Beautiful! I loved it. This was one of the classic miracles. Close with commentary.

Yehuda: There you have it. Joshua Ben-Nun has split the Jordan River with the help of God and the Israelites are now in the land of Canaan. It was a splendid day for Israel. Barbara, any final words?

Barbara: The monument of the twelve stones is a wonderful touch. It's set up in the perfect spot for a day trip with the family. I guess the big question on the mind of all Israelites right now would have to be, "What am I going to wear to the Battle of Jericho?"

Director: Okay and fade out.

THE WALLS OF JERICHO
Joshua 6

Boy: Programs, get your programs. The Israelite parade should start in just a few minutes.

Person 1: Tickets are getting harder to find each day.

Person 2: This is my first show. What have I been missing?

Person 1: Well, the Israelites march around the city of Jericho every day with seven priests carrying seven ram's horns. In back of the priests is their Holy Ark. It's a great parade. They've been doing it for six days.

Servant: Make way for the King of Jericho.

King: Hello, everybody. It's your wonderful king who sacrifices little children and worships idols. I hope you're enjoying the show.

Servant: Your majesty, aren't you a little worried about the Israelites?

King: In case you haven't noticed, we have an inpenetrable wall between us and them. If they think that marching around Jericho is scaring us, we fooled them. This is the best show in town. We're making a fortune on tickets and concessions.

Servant: I have to admit, this is the hottest program since sacrificing those maidens from Ashdod last year.

King: I love the noise. I love the horn bands. They have such natural rhythm. People are starting to hum their tunes in the streets. They call it the Israelite Ramtime Blues.

Person 1: Look, the Israelites are going to march around the city a second time today.

Person 2: Wow, a doubleheader. For six days, they circled the city once. Today is the first time they've done it more than once.

Servant: The crowd is ecstatic! Hey, shouldn't we be charging them more for a doubleheader?

King: No. We'll make it up in concession sales.

Person 1: Seven times around the city! I love it.

Person 2: Look, the Israelites have stopped and Joshua is stepping forward.

Joshua: Shout! The Lord has given you the city. The city and everything in it are set aside for the Lord. Only Rahab is to be spared along with all who are in her house.

King: What in Baal is he talking about?

Joshua: Do not take anything that is set aside for the Lord or there will be trouble.

King: Oh, I get it. Joshua is doing a stand up comedy routine. Let's hear some heckling.

Person 1: You bet there will be trouble. Hey, Joshua — how are you going to get over our wall — pole vault?

Joshua: All the silver and gold and objects of copper and iron are consecrated to the Lord. They must go into the treasury of the Lord.

Person 2: It's nice of this guy to give away *my* jewelry.

Joshua: Shout!

King: This is incredible. Seven times around the city and now the Israelites are shouting and blowing the horns. Plus Joshua gives a stand-up routine. Advance ticket sales for tomorrow's show are going to sky rocket.

Person 1: Hey, quit shaking the bleachers.

Person 2: I thought you were shaking the bleachers.

Servant: Your majesty. What plans do we have for earthquakes?

King: No refunds.

Servant: The walls of Jericho are tumbling down!

King: Let's get out of here.

Narrator: And the Israelites rushed into Jericho and everything in the city fell by the sword. And Joshua bade the two men who spied out the land to bring out Rahab.

Spy 1: Knock, knock.

Rahab: Nobody's home.

Spy 2: Rahab, it's the spies. You can come out now.

Rahab: Nobody's home.

Spy 1: Rahab, we are the guys who pledged our lives to protect you. We told you to tie a crimson cord outside your window to warn the Israelites not to attack this place. Open up.

Rahab: Any Tom, Dick, or Chaim could have known that. But I still recognize your awful accents. We're saved! Come on in. This is ma, pa, the brothers, the sisters, the extended family, the goats, the cows, and the kids.

Narrator: And the spies brought Rahab and her family out and they were spared, along with all that belonged to her, and she dwelt with the Israelites. And Joshua said . . .

Joshua: Cursed be anyone who tries to refortify Jericho. It will be at a terrible cost.

Narrator: And real estate values dipped dramatically in Jericho.

THE BATTLE FOR AI

Joshua 7-8

Spy 1: Joshua, good news. The city of Ai is not that tough a place.

Spy 2: There's no need to shlep the entire army to Ai. We can probably get away with about two or three thousand warriors.

Joshua: That's good news. After destroying Jericho, we can use an easy battle. And you are right. If we have the whole gang go up to Ai to fight a small army, the complaints will be louder than the shouting at Jericho.

Narrator: Three thousand of the troops went up to attack Ai and they were defeated by the men of Ai. The men of Ai pursued them as far as Shebarim.

Joshua: Lord, woe is to us. First You take us out of Egypt, lead us through the desert for forty years, give us the Ten Commandments, and cross us over the Jordan River only to be defeated by Amorites! We should never have crossed the Jordan.

God: Let's not overreact.

Joshua: But if the Canaanites hear about this defeat, they will turn on us and wipe out our very name from the earth.

God: Joshua, this is only one setback and you deserved it. Israel sinned. You broke the covenant by taking spoils in Jericho. Israel will not be able to defeat its enemies until the perpetrators are caught. Now find those who are ruining things for Israel.

* * *

Holmes: Inspector Holmes reporting for duty.

Joshua: Excellent. We have assembled the twelve tribes. Which tribe stole the spoils from Jericho?

Holmes: Elementary, my dear Joshua. The tribe of Judah is guilty. There's whispering going on which indicates indubitably that they have something to hide.

Joshua: All other tribes can leave except Judah. Now, Holmes, how can we figure out which clan in the tribe did it?

Holmes: Joshua, must I do all your work? Zerah is guilty. I detect a smoky odor indicating spoils from the burnt city of Jericho.

Joshua: Amazing. Very well, all clans except Zerah may go.

Holmes: One of your families in this clan is guilty. Not only did you steal the spoils of Jericho, but you caused Israel to be defeated by Ai, a pip-squeak of a town. Where's my spy glass? Nobody leaves until the mystery is solved.

Achan: I can't stand the tension any longer. I confess. I did it. I saw the mantle and two hundred shekels of silver and the wedge of gold and I figured . . . who's gonna miss it? I buried it in my tent. Forgive me.

Holmes: There we have it. Mystery solved. I shall call it "The Case of Achan's Agony."

Achan: Will I be forgiven?

Joshua: Take Achan and his family and all his belongings including his stolen spoils and bring them to the Valley of Achor where they will be put to fire and stoned to death.

Achan: Shall I take that as a no?

Narrator: And all Israel pelted him with stones. They raised a huge mound of stones over him, which is still there, and the anger of the Lord subsided.

*   *   *

God: Joshua, return to Ai with your fighting troops and I will now deliver the city into your hands.

17

Joshua: I'm a little nervous about this. Last time, we blew it. Those guys are tough . . . good defense, adequate offense.

God: This time, you will set an ambush.

Joshua: That's going to do it? An ambush?

God: And take an extra thirty thousand valiant men.

Joshua: That'll do it.

Narrator: And Joshua instructed five thousand men to lay in ambush, west of the city.

Advisor: Sire, Joshua and his men choose to do battle with us again.

King of Ai: Let's finish them off this time. Get the entire armed forces — every last soldier, sailor, marine — and we'll chase them back to the Jordan.

Advisor: The soldiers and marines are here, but we may have trouble rounding up the sailors. The navy has been a problem.

King of Ai: What is the matter with our navy?

Advisor: To begin with — we are a landlocked nation.

King of Ai: Very well. Nix the Navy. Get the cheerleaders down here. Charge!

Advisor: Sire, look . . . Joshua and his army have turned and are running.

King of Ai: Chickens. They're chickens. Cluck cluck cluck.

Narrator: And the Lord told Joshua to point his javelin toward Ai. And Joshua did so, signaling the ambush to attack the city. And the city had been left completely open.

King of Ai: Excuse me, but why do you think the Israelites

18

have stopped running and have turned to face us?

Advisor: I'd be a liar, sire, if I said I knew. But they don't look chicken anymore.

King of Ai: Let's slowly turn around and run for Ai as fast as we can.

Advisor: Uh oh. The city is on fire, sire. Didn't you close the front gate?

King of Ai: No, I thought you closed the front gate. Now, what do we do? We have Israelites in front of us, and oops . . . we have Israelites behind us.

Advisor: Not wishing to tire my sire, my advice is simple: "Aiiii . . . . Everyone for himself."

Narrator: And Israel killed all the inhabitants of Ai who had run into the wilderness . . . every last warrior. Ai was put to the sword. And Joshua did not draw back the hand with which he held out the javelin until all of Ai was defeated.

Israelite: Joshua, God's work is done. Ai is no more.

Joshua: Well, it's about time. My arm is stiffer than an ironing board. What took you so long? Never mind. Just gather up all the people.

Narrator: And all Israel stood on either side of the Ark. They offered sacrifices of well-being. Half of the people faced Mount Ebal and half faced Mount Gerizim and, as Moses the servant of the Lord had commanded them of old, they blessed the people of Israel.

Joshua: Now, I know we've had some rough times. Walking around Jericho was no picnic. The town of Ai was tougher than we thought. We're all a little tired and grumpy. So it's time to remind ourselves of why we're here.

Israelite: Get comfortable. This is going to take a while.

Joshua: I am now going to read you the words of the Teaching, including the blessings and curses. I will not skip a word that Moses wrote down.

Israelite: I knew I should have worn my comfortable sandals.

Narrator: And Joshua read all the words which Moses had commanded in the presence of the entire assembly of Israel, including the women and the children and the strangers that accompanied them.

TALES OF GIBEON
Joshua 9-12

Gibeonite 1: How does my disguise look?

Gibeonite 2: Great. I love your threadbare clothes.

Gibeonite 1: It's not too much, is it? We're supposed to look like we live in the desert and have been walking for days.

Gibeonite 2: It's perfect. And look at my worn out sandals. The wardrobe people outdid themselves.

Gibeonite 3: The mules are ready. Even they are seedy looking.

Gibeonite 2: I like the worn out sacks on their backs, but the "Gilgal or Bust" sign might be overdoing it.

Gibeonite 3: This has got to be perfect in order to fool the Israelites. Everything is ready. Let's go to Gilgal and meet Joshua.

Israelite 1: Hark, I see strangers coming. They look tired and poor.

Joshua: Greetings, strangers.

Gibeonite 1: Greetings, O mighty one, O powerful leader.

Gibeonite 2: Oh, be quiet. Joshua, we come from a distant land and we propose to make a pact with you.

Israelite 2: How do we know you are not from around here?

Gibeonite 3: Take a look at our props, uh . . . costumes, uh . . . worn clothes. We come from a very distant land.

Gibeonite 1: Very, very distant. Even far away.

Gibeonite 3: We will be your subjects. We heard of you because of the fame of your Lord who brought you out of Egypt and helped you defeat your enemies east of the Jordan.

Gibeonite 2: Look at this bread. It was still hot when we started our journey. Now it's just dry crumbs. And look at our clothes. We're disgusting. We've been on the road for a long, long time.

Joshua: We shall make a friendship pact with you. Your lives will be spared. You have our oath.

Gibeonite 2: Farewell, our friends and allies.

Gibeonite 3: We did it! They fell for the old dry breadcrumb routine.

Narrator: Three days passed and the Israelites learned that the so-called strangers were really neighbors who lived close by. So the Israelites set out and in three days came to their towns of Gibeon, Chephirah, Beeroth, and Kiriath-Jearim.

Israelite 1: Those Gibeonites tricked us. The scoundrels.

Narrator: And the whole Israelite community muttered against the Gibeonites.

Israelites: Mutter, mutter, mutter.

Narrator: But the chieftains answered that the Israelites had sworn an oath and, therefore, could not touch them. So Joshua summoned the Gibeonites.

Joshua: Why did you trick us and say you lived in a distant land?

Gibeonite 2: Three days is distant. Sort of. All right, it's not China, but it's not next door, either.

Gibeonite 1: Joshua, what would you have done to us had you come to our cities?

Joshua: We would have attacked your city, burned it to the ground, and destroyed all the inhabitants.

Gibeonite 3: So our choices are total destruction or working for you as servants. Let's face it, considering what you did to Jericho, what choice did we have? You do not have a reputation for being very merciful. Do what you must.

Joshua: You shall become hewers of wood and drawers of water for Israel.

Gibeonite 1: We can live with that.

* * *

Narrator: When King Adoni-tzedek of Jerusalem heard that Joshua had captured Ai, treating it as he had Jericho, and that the people of Gibeon had come to terms with Israel, he was frightened. He sent messengers out to the kings of Hebron, Eglon, Lachish, and Jarmuth.

Messenger: Joshua, I bring a message from Gibeon.

Joshua: What is it now? Are they going to try to sell us some swampland?

Messenger: O mighty leader, O great warrior, O Joshua . . .

Joshua: O, get on with it.

Messenger: The five Amorite kings of the hill country have gathered an army against us. Do not fail your servants who, by the way, love hewing wood and drawing water for you. Help us.

Joshua: Five kings? I wonder why they'd be angry with Gibeon. They are such lovable people.

Messenger: That will be ten shekels. The Gibeonites sent the message C.O.D.

Narrator: Joshua marched up from Gilgal with his whole

force, all the trained warriors. And Joshua took the armies of the five kings by surprise.

Israelite 2: Joshua, the armies are fleeing from us.

Israelite 1: We need more time and weapons to cut them down.

Israelite 2: Perhaps not. Look, huge stones are falling from the skies. They're destroying more of the enemy than our weapons.

Joshua: We still need more time. Just one big miracle. Let there be light!

Israelite 1: Hey, that's God's line.

Joshua: Stand still, O sun, at Gibeon, O moon, in the Valley of Aijalon.

Israelite 1: Check this out. The sun stands still. Daylight savings time to the max!

Narrator: Thus the sun halted in mid-heaven and did not set for a whole day, for the Lord fought for Israel. Neither before nor since has there been such a day when the Lord acted on words spoken by a man.

Israelite 2: Joshua, we found the five kings hiding in a cave. And we rolled a stone in front of the entrance. What do you want to do with them?

Joshua: Well, we're not going to invite them for dinner.

Narrator: And Joshua captured many kings and towns and put them to the sword. Thus he conquered the entire hill country. And King Jabin of Hazor gathered the kings throughout Canaan and they met Joshua and the Israelites in battle and were defeated. In total, Joshua fought and defeated thirty-one kings, which is a bunch. When the country was conquered, the land had rest from war. Everybody was pretty exhausted.

DIVIDING THE LAND —
REAL ESTATE RED TAG SALE
Joshua 13-19

Person 1: Canaan Real Estate Company, please hold. Canaan Real Estate, be with you in a minute. Could I have some help up here? The phones are ringing off the hook.

Person 2: You think you have problems. There is a line around the block. Everybody wants to sell their land before the Israelites attack and take over.

Person 1: The Israelites have everyone going crazy. Land hasn't been this cheap since the great flood.

Person 2: I've heard that the Israelites haven't been able to drive out everyone. The Philistines and Sidonians aren't moving.

Person 1: But those are tough neighborhoods. Who would want to move there? Back to the phones. Canaan Real Estate Company, may we help you?

* * *

Narrator: And Joshua was now old and advanced in years. And the Lord told Joshua that though all the land was not yet conquered, the territory was to be divided into portions for nine of the tribes.

Joshua: Eleazar, as High Priest, you have the honor of helping me and the chieftains assign the portions of land for each tribe.

Eleazar: Are you sure this is an honor? The people are making some pretty heavy requests. This tribe wants beach front property. Another tribe wants mountains with a river view. This is not going to be fun.

25

Joshua: It's a tough job, but someone's gotta do it.

Eleazar: Okay, everyone, calm down, quiet. We have a tough day ahead of us.

Joshua: Reuben, Gad, and Manasseh, you've been given the land east of the Jordan as was promised to you by Moses.

Eleazar: Three down and nine to go. Now, what do we do?

Caleb: Joshua! Can I have a word with you?

Eleazar: I didn't know Caleb was still alive. He's one of the original people who left Egypt. He's ancient. He's old . . . a dinosaur.

Joshua: He's my age. We left Egypt together.

Eleazar: And what a fine looking senior citizen he is.

Caleb: Joshua, I have come to claim the land Moses promised me for being a loyal spy. The other ten spies were cowardly, but you and I gave brave and honest reports. God has preserved me as was promised. I was 40 years old when I was sent out as a spy and it's been 45 years since God made that promise to me.

Eleazar: Eighty-five years old! You don't look a day over seventy.

Caleb: I'm still as strong today as on the day Moses sent me. Give me the hill country near Hebron and I'll conquer the Anakites who occupy the land. You may as well assign Judah to be around there with me.

Joshua: Are you sure they'll go?

Caleb: By the time they decide whether they want beach front or mountain view, their grandchildren will have grand-children.

Narrator: So Joshua assigned land in the south to the tribe of Judah, and Caleb was among the tribe of Judah. And to the tribes of Joseph, Joshua assigned the hill country.

Eleazar: Five down and seven to go. Uh, oh. Here come the leaders of Ephraim and Manasseh. They are such complainers.

Manasseh: Joshua, why have you assigned us one allotment when we are two tribes and a numerous people?

Eleazar: Gripe, gripe, gripe. Does this look like the complaint window? I told you these guys were never satisfied.

Ephraim: The hill country is not enough.

Eleazar: Kvetch, kvetch.

Joshua: Very well, you are indeed numerous. You shall also be given the forest country to the north.

Manasseh: But the Canaanites that live there have iron chariots.

Joshua: Even though they have iron chariots, you will be able to dispossess the Canaanites.

Narrator: And Joshua sent out men to traverse the land. They documented all of Canaan and divided it into seven parts for the remaining tribes. Joshua then cast lots and parcelled out the land according to the divisions. And the Israelites gave a portion of land in their midst to Joshua.

THE LAST DAYS OF JOSHUA

Joshua 20-24

Joshua: Well, that does it. No more screaming and yelling about who gets what. The land is distributed.

Eleazar: Ahem, ahem.

Joshua: Now, I can go settle down on the farm and live out the rest of the years of my life. Time for fishing and . . .

Eleazar: Ahem, ahem.

Joshua: Yeah, the land is in our hands, give or take a few places. Let's close down this operation. I'm pooped.

Eleazar: Ahem, ahem.

Joshua: Do you have cold, Eleazar?

Eleazar: Joshua, you seem to be ignoring the fact that there are an awful lot of people still standing around waiting for some decisions to be made.

Joshua: We have given out all the land. We have twelve tribes and they all have land. You, out there, shoo. Go home to the lands you were given.

Eleazar: You gave land to every tribe but one . . .

Joshua: Oh, yeah? Oops, I'm sorry, Eleazar. I forgot your tribe — the Levites. And they've been so polite while they've waited.

Narrator: Joshua commanded the Israelites to assign cities out of their land for the Levites. And the Israelites designated certain cities as cities of refuge.

Joshua: Goodbye, everyone. See ya, Eleazar.

Secretary: Joshua, there are quite a few people still here.

Joshua: What do you mean? I have given the Levites their cities. Did we grow another tribe or something?

Secretary: They're men from Reuben, Gad, and the half tribe of Manasseh.

Joshua: Tell them they can go.

Secretary: They won't leave until you say the magic word. I pulled the file for you. Here's what you said to them, and I quote, "Leave your wives and children in this territory assigned to you. Your fighting men shall go across armed in the company of your kinsmen. You shall assist them until the land is in their possession. Then you may return to the territory on the east side of the Jordan that Moses assigned to you." Wow, we were pretty tough on these guys.

Joshua: Reuben, Gad, and Manasseh, thank you. You can go home now.

Reuben: That's it? Twenty years of fighting. Eating in the mess tents. Battling countless enemies. And you say, "You can go home now"?

Narrator: And Joshua blessed them saying, "Return to your homes with great wealth — quantities of gold, silver, iron, and copper, and with a great quantity of clothing. Share the spoils of our enemies with your kinsmen. But remember to fulfill the Instruction and Teaching that Moses, the servant of the Lord, commanded unto you."

Reuben: Now, that's much better.

* * *

Narrator: Many years passed and Joshua was old and he assembled all Israel, their elders, commanders, magistrates, and officials at Shechem.

Manager: Shechem Motel. Yes, we are filled. Shechem Motel,

I'm sorry, no vacancies. Boy, this is incredible.

Clerk: Business is pretty good, huh, boss?

Manager: Unbelievable. Everybody's here for Joshua's farewell address. Tonight, he is making a covenant for the people. We had better get there early.

Clerk: Don't worry, boss. I parked my camels real close to the stage. Good seats are guaranteed.

Narrator: And Joshua spoke to all the people at Shechem.

Joshua: Be mindful to love the Lord. Do not mingle with the nations left among you. They can be a trap. Keep the covenant and none of the good things that God promised you will fail to happen.

Israelite 1: That's cool.

Joshua: If you break the covenant and serve other gods, then the Lord's anger will burn against you and you shall perish from the good land God has given you.

Israelite 2: Wow, that's tough. Keep the covenant and be rewarded. Break it and perish. Such a choice. What is an Israelite to do!

Joshua: Oops, I lost my place. Have I told you about Abraham, Isaac, and Jacob?

Israelite 3: About three hours ago.

Joshua: What about Moses and Aaron?

Israelite 2: You have retold the entire history of our people. Have mercy! No more reruns.

Joshua: I'm coming down the homestretch. Do not forsake the Lord.

Israelites: We promise.

Joshua: Scout's honor?

Narrator: And after these events, Joshua son of Nun died at the age of one hundred and ten years. And the bones of Joseph which were brought from Egypt were buried in Shechem. And Eleazar son of Aaron also died, and they buried him in the hills of Ephraim.

THE ISRAELITES SETTLE IN

Judges 2:6-3:14

Narrator: Joshua dismissed the people. The Israelites went to their allotted territories and occupied the land. However, they were not able to dispossess completely the inhabitants. And another generation arose after Joshua and they worshiped idols, forsaking God.

Messenger: Knock, knock.

Israel: Go away, we're busy praying to the idols of the peoples around us.

Messenger: Special delivery for the tribes of Israel.

Israel: We can't be bothered right now. We're forsaking the Lord in order to follow Baal, god of the Canaanites.

Messenger: You might want to hear this message. You have provoked the Almighty and you shall be punished.

Israel: This is going to hurt, isn't it?

Messenger: If you already know the answer, you might as well not ask the question. The Almighty is handing you over to your enemies. You won't stand a chance. They're going to defeat you in battle, make you pay heavy taxes, force you to be slaves . . . and that isn't the half of it.

Israelites: Woe to us. We have sinned.

Messenger: You ain't just a whistling Dixie.

Narrator: But God heard the cries of the people and raised up warrior chieftains who delivered them from their enemies.

Israelites: We promise we'll never stray again.

Messenger: Never say never.

Narrator: And the Israelites would again act wickedly after their chieftan was gone.

Messenger: Knock, knock.

Israel: Who is it? We're very busy bowing to other gods and being even worse than our ancestors.

Messenger: It's a messenger from God.

Israel: Which one? Baal? Ashterah? George Burns?

Messenger: The One and only God. You're in trouble again.

Israel: Woe to us. We have sinned.

Messenger: Talk about a broken record. God has decided not to give over all of Canaan to you. The other nations will stay here and live among you. They will be a test of your faith to God. You had better change your evil ways.

Israel: Woe to us. We have sinned.

Messenger: And you're lousy tippers, to boot!

EHUD, THE LEFT-HANDED
Judges 3:12-3:30

Teacher: All right, class. It's time to open our texts for another lesson about Judges.

Joey: Oh, boy. My favorite subject . . . Bible. It's right up there with detention and extra homework.

Hilda: What will happen this week? Let me guess. The Israelites will do evil things and . . .

Jeff: God will get real mad and some king of the Aramites or the Moabites or some other "ite" will conquer the Israelites, who will then promise not to sin anymore.

Helga: Woe to us. We have sinned.

Teacher: Class, we have been studying about the judges who arose to save the Israelites. They were brave people.

Joey: I've got to get out of here.

Teacher: Today, we'll look at Ehud of Benjamin whose tribe had been enslaved by the Moabites. He used a very interesting strategy to free his people. Anybody want to guess? Joey, your hand is up.

Joey: Bathroom?

Teacher: Excellent answer. How did you know?

Joey: Huh?

Teacher: He used the bathroom.

Joey: Maybe, I'll stay for this story. You were saying, Teach?

* * *

34

Benjy 1: Ehud, what are we going to do? King Eglon is oppressing our tribe, as well as other tribes.

Ehud: Trust me. I have a plan. I will deliver our people's taxes to the king. But not only will I bring him money, I will also bring him a special surprise. This dagger.

Benjy 2: I hate to be a spoil sport, Ehud, but have you ever seen King Eglon?

Ehud: Not really.

Benjy 1: If you stab him with that dagger, he's going to think that a mosquito bit him. This is one large king.

Benjy 2: We are talking "very stout." You know how most kings are carried around on their portable thrones by four guys? Well, Eglon needs ten slaves plus a crew of substitutes tagging behind in case someone passes out.

Ehud: So, a little dagger isn't going to do much. There goes my plan.

Benjy 1: How about using this two-edged dagger? It's a full cubit long.

Ehud: Where did you get that?

Benjy 1: I bought it for when my mother-in-law comes to visit. Since I purchased it, we never fight anymore.

Ehud: Well, ready or not, let's go meet the king.

Courtesan: Hear ye, hear ye. The court of King Eglon of Moab is now in session.

Ehud: What's that rumble? Holy Moly, dive for cover, it's an earthquake!

Benjy 1: Ehud, get up. That's not an earthquake. It's just King Eglon coming into the room.

Eglon: Who wishes to approach me today?

Ehud: Your largeness . . . I mean, your bigness . . . I mean . . . King Eglon, it is I, Ehud the left-handed Benjaminite. I bring you the tribute you have mercilessly demanded from my people.

Eglon: Do you have anything to eat in that chest?

Ehud: No, just gold and silver from poor suffering shepherds.

Eglon: Spare me the sob story. A man's gotta eat.

Courtesan: Another cow, your majesty?

Eglon: Five's enough for one meal. I'm dieting. Now, if you'll excuse me. I have to go you know where.

Ehud: But, King Eglon, I bring you a secret message.

Eglon: All right. But you'll have to come with me. Nature is calling. Now, then. What is your business?

Ehud: I bring you a divine message.

Eglon: Hey, what are you doing with that dagger? If you need to wash first, just say so. Ahhhhhhh.

Servant: Where is King Eglon?

Ehud: He must still be in his cooling chambers. They're locked and closed shut.

Courtesan: Well, he did have a big lunch.

* * *

Teacher: And Ehud escaped from the castle and sounded the ram's horn throughout the hill country and Israelites rallied to his side. While the Moabites waited for their fallen leader, the Israelites attacked and defeated their army. And Moab surrendered to Israel.

Helga: Until the next time . . . when they all start sinning again.

Joey: Now that's what I call a great piece of literature, teacher.

WOMEN WAGE WAR

Judges 4:1-5:31

Lapidoth: Deborah, your next appointment is here.

Deborah: How many more are there?

Lapidoth: They're lined up halfway to Bethel. Plus you're getting letters by the goatskin and you've been invited to speak at the Wolf's Club in Benjamin and at the Old Olive Press in Asher. You're quite a good judge, honey.

Deborah: Shhh. You don't call the leader of the Israelites "honey."

Lapidoth: I can't help it. You make me so proud sitting under that palm tree of yours making all those wise decisions. I may be your agent, but I'm also your husband. Kissy, kissy.

Deborah: Quit talking gushy to the judge. Call in the next case.

Woman: Oh, wise Deborah who sits under the palm tree. My best friend has taken the quilt that I was making and has given it to her husband.

Friend: That's not true. It is my quilt. She is just jealous that I can sew so well. She can only sew, so so.

Deborah: Let me see the quilt. I guess I'll just have to cut it in half and give part of it to each of you.

Woman: That sounds fair.

Friend: Sure. Go for it.

Deborah: That's not the way it's supposed to work. Oh well, rip it.

All: Ooh, ahh. What a great judge.

Deborah: Some days are strange . . . but, this sure beats standing over a hot bonfire cooking blintz soufflé. Next!

Warrior: Oh, wise Deborah who sits under the palm tree.

Lapidoth: I told you this palm tree was a great touch, honey.

Deborah: I am trying to listen to the nice warrior. Say, who does your outfits? I love the colors.

Warrior: Deborah, we have been oppressed by King Jabin of Canaan for twenty years. Israel has repented for its sins. We must rise up and fight for our freedom. God will be with us.

Deborah: Well, you're the warrior. Go get 'em.

Warrior: King Jabin and his general Sisera have nine hundred iron chariots.

Deborah: How many do we have?

Warrior: None.

Deborah: It could be worse. We have goodness and faith on our side.

Warrior: A real superbowl. Nine hundred chariots versus goodness and faith!

Deborah: All right, I'll take care of this problem. Have you contacted Shamgar, the judge from down south? He slew six hundred Philistines with an ox goad.

Lapidoth: Shamgar died about fifty years ago.

Deborah: And nobody told me. Do we have a communications glitch or what? Find me Barak from the tribe of Naphtali. I remember him from my last speaking gig up there.

Lapidoth: Deborah, if you take time out for this war, we're going to have to cancel a lot of talk shows and celebrity interviews.

Deborah: A woman's gotta do what a woman's gotta do. And by the way, Lapidoth, you'll have to clean the tent while I'm off fighting this war.

Barak: Deborah, I have come as you have summoned me.

Deborah: Whew, that was fast! Barak, the Lord has commanded that you take ten thousand men of Naphtali and Zebulun and march them to Mount Tabor.

Barak: What about reenforcements?

Deborah: No one else is coming.

Barak: Why not?

Deborah: Oh, something about the enemy having nine hundred chariots. Now, the plan is for me to draw Sisera and his army into the river bed where you'll smash them.

Barak: Excuse me . . . did you say, nine hundred chariots?

Deborah: Barak, you can do it. Sure, it requires planning. But if I can lead the nation, serve as its judge, and still have time to clean the tent, put a decent meal on the table, and milk the goats, I think that a trained warrior like you can cut through the minor problem of a few hundred chariots. Now, let's win this one so I can get back to my career.

* * *

Servant: Sisera, the Israelites are mounting an attack.

Sisera: Who's leading them?

Servant: Barak and Deborah.

Sisera: A woman! Well, pass out the powder puffs and let's go to war.

40

Narrator: And Barak charged down from Mount Tabor, followed by ten thousand men, and the army of Sisera was thrown into disarray. Sisera leapt from his chariot and fled on foot.

Sisera: A tent, at last.

Jael: Come in, my lord. I am Jael, the Kenite. You must be tired after running from battle. What's the matter?

Sisera: Defeated by a woman. I can't believe it. She had a lot of luck. All of our chariots got stuck in the riverbed.

Jael: And, naturally, you had chosen the riverbed to be the battlefield.

Sisera: No, the Israelites did. What luck they had.

Jael: Yeah, especially to have a general like you on the other side.

Sisera: What?

Jael: Nothing. You're falling asleep. It must have been the milk I gave you. Rest now . . . and I'll take care of your headache.

Sisera: But I don't have a headache.

Jael: You will.

Narrator: Hey, boys and girls. Life in the time of the Judges was not always easy. Let's just say that Jael killed General Sisera and if you are really interested in details you can look it up in Judges 4:21. Shhh. Don't tell your little brothers and sisters.

Barak: Hello. Is anyone home?

Jael: Barak, it is I, Jael the Kenite, friend of the Israelites.

Barak: Have you seen Sisera? We've defeated his army and he escaped.

41

Jael: Search no further. Behold, Sisera is in my tent . . . taking a permanent rest.

Barak: Well, I'll be . . . Jael and Deborah, you have defeated the Canaanites.

Deborah: Ah, well, a woman's work is never done. Nine hundred chariots? It was nothing compared to being a housewife and a judge of Israel. Now that's a challenge.

GIDEON IS CHOSEN

Judges 6:1-6:32

Announcer: We take you now inside the Midianite army camp where we have secretly replaced all peace loving people with complete barbarians. Let's listen in on their idle conversation.

Midianite 1: Coffee, Sir? It's decaf.

Midianite 2: Mmmm. Thanks. After a full day of invading the Israelites and pillaging the countryside, this really hits the spot.

Midianite 3: Let's go make some more Israelites miserable. This is more fun than riding wild camels.

Midianite 2: Well, I just came from a meeting. There's good news and bad news. The generals say that we have to allow the Israelites to sow their land and let their crops start to grow.

Midianite 1: What a bummer! What's the good news?

Midianite 2: Just when they think they'll get to harvest their crops, we destroy all their produce.

Midianite 1: I love it. More coffee, anyone?

Announcer: Excuse me, Mr. Midianite General.

General: You can call me "Butcher."

Announcer: What if we were to tell you that we had secretly replaced some of your more peace loving soldiers with total barbarians.

General: I can't believe it.

Announcer: Well, we did.

43

General: No wonder they're such good fighters. From now on, all of our soldiers will be barbarians. Let's go steal all the Israelite cows and sheep. But first . . . let's have another cup of coffee.

Prophet: God, do I really have to do this?

God: Yes, my people are once again suffering and I want them to know that it is because they are not obeying Me and are worshiping other gods.

Prophet: But they never listen. Could You send someone else? I know you want Israel to repent, but I've got to pick up groceries, tidy up the sand in front of my tent, and so much more.

God: And with whom are you speaking?

Prophet: That's an easy question. I'm talking with the God of Israel, who redeemed Israel from Egypt, who split the Sea of Reeds, who defeated our enemies, and who gave us this land, who is the most powerful . . . let me read over my assignment again. I'm on my way.

Announcer: And an angel of the Lord came and sat under the terebinth of Ophrah.

Gideon: (sings) "I've been working on the winepress all the live-long day. Keeping produce from the Midianites by hiding it in the hay."

Angel: Excuse me, I heard your singing. I'm looking for Gideon.

Gideon: Are you an agent? Are you going to give me my big break?

Angel: In a way. God is with you, valiant warrior.

Gideon: Really? You wouldn't be talking about the Lord who took us out of Egypt and abandoned us to the Midianites?

Angel: That's why I've come to you. You are from a great tribe.

Gideon: Manasseh is a nice tribe, but nobody's ever called us great.

Angel: You're from a well known family.

Gideon: Be serious. We're the bottom of the barrel.

Angel: How about the fact that you're a future leader of your household?

Gideon: Actually, I'm the youngest son. I'll be lucky to inherit the rooster.

Angel: Okay. So I didn't brush up on your bio. You have been chosen to free Israel from the Midianites.

Gideon: I need a sign. Something to back up what you're saying.

Angel: Proof? You want proof? Where did I put that book? Here it is. "Minor Miracles for the Amateur Angel." Uh huh. Rods into serpents. That's been done. Ooh, here's one. Make a stew and put it over there on the rock.

Gideon: A stew. I ask for a sign from God and get helpful hints from Betty Crocker. Okay. There's the stew. I hope this works.

Angel: You and me both.

Announcer: And a fire sprang up from the rock and consumed the stew.

Angel: And now for the grand finale. Ta dah.

Gideon: Wow! He completely disappeared.

Angel: Harry Houdini, eat your heart out.

* * *

Announcer: That night, God commanded Gideon to tear down the evil altar to Baal and build an altar to Adonai.

Israelite 1: Joash, bring your son out here. He's ruined our altar.

Israelite 2: What are you going to do about it?

Joash: I could take away his allowance.

Israelite 3: He must die. He has torn down the altar of Baal.

Joash: If Baal is so mad with Gideon, let Baal kill my son himself.

Gideon: Gee, thanks, dad. Anything to save on my allowance.

Israelite 1: Joash is right. If Baal wants his altar, he can take care of it himself.

Announcer: And the people gave Gideon a new name, Jerubaal, meaning "Let Baal contend with him," since he tore down the altar of Baal.

Gideon: The new name is okay, but you guys can still call me Gideon for short.

GIDEON'S BATTLE
Judges 6:33-7:8

Narrator: The spirit of the Lord enveloped Gideon. He sounded the horn and the people of his clan and his tribe rallied to his side. Gideon sent out messengers to the tribes of Asher, Naphtali, and Zebulun.

Gideon: How's the crowd out there, Shirley?

Shirley: Everyone is real excited. Who doesn't love a concert? That horn of yours is making you famous.

Gideon: I only hope that they listen to what I have to say.

Shirley: Oh, Mr. Gideon. If anyone can talk them into fighting the Midianites, I'm sure it's you.

Gideon: Citizens of Israel. I say to you tonight that we've got tzorus. That's trouble with a "Tzee" that rhymes with "Me" and that stands for Midian.

Shirley: Wow, he's on a roll.

Gideon: Now, I can tell you are all good God-fearing people who don't worship idols, and you want to rid the land of the evil Midianites. Well, I'm showing you a way to cleanse yourselves of the no good, rotten enemies of Israel. I say we've got tzorus.

All: Yes, we have tzorus.

Gideon: Right here in Israel.

All: Right here in Israel.

Gideon: We've got tzorus with a "Tzee" that rhymes with "Me" and that stands for Midian.

47

All: Tzorus, tzorus, tzorus.

Shirley: I love this part. Here comes the horn. And the crowd goes crazy.

Gideon: Shirley, we're a hit. Post the sign-up sheets out there, and I'll be right back.

Shirley: You're not going to your tent for more proof from God, are you?

Gideon: There's nothing wrong with being sure.

Shirley: You're meshugah. That starts with "M" that rhymes with "N" which stands for noodge. Two nights ago you asked God for proof by placing a rug down and saying you'll believe if the next day you find that the ground is dry, but there is dew on the rug. And . . .

Gideon: And God did so.

Shirley: So, then you ask God for proof by saying you'll believe if the next day the ground around the rug is wet, but the rug is dry. And God does it. Look, Gideon, you're really pushing it. What now? Wet rug and wet ground? How about oatmeal cookies under everyone's pillows?

Gideon: Great idea. I'll go ask God.

Soldier: Sorry to interrupt, but all the volunteers are assembled.

Gideon: How many have joined the army?

Soldier: Let me see . . . eggs, lentil beans, goat milk . . . oops, that's the shopping list. Here it is. The grand total is 32,000.

Gideon: Well, what are we waiting for? Let's go fight the Midianites.

Shirley: What about asking God for another proof of faith?

Gideon: Shirley, are you doubting the Lord? Look at me. I now have total faith. Of course, 32,000 men doesn't hurt.

Narrator: The next day, Jerubbaal . . .

Gideon: But you can call me Gideon.

Narrator: We'll try it again. The next day, Jerubbaal, that is Gideon, and all his troops pitched camp above En-harod while the Midianite army was to the north.

God: Gideon.

Gideon: Lord, we are ready. Let's go after those Midianite meatballs.

God: You have too many troops.

Gideon: One can never have too much of a good thing.

God: If you attack now, Israel might think that the victory is theirs and that it is not due to God's help.

Gideon: I'll talk to each one of them personally and get a written guarantee on sheepskin that they won't think that. Please.

God: Send them home.

Gideon: May I have everyone's attention? Anyone who is the least bit scared of getting hurt has permission to go home.

God: Gideon, there are still too many troops.

Gideon: What can I say? They're a great bunch of fellas.

God: You have more troops than we need.

Gideon: But ten thousand is such a nice round number. Okay, so how many do we need in order to fight the gigantic, brutal, Midianite army?

God: Three hundred men should do it.

Gideon: Three hundred? As in three zero zero? It'll take a miracle to defeat the Midianites with only three hundred.

God: Exactly.

General: Okay, we have to narrow our army down. Therefore, Gideon has devised a test from God. First, let's all go down to the river and take a drink of water.

Gideon: Now this is tricky. You have to write down the names of everyone who laps the water out of their hands rather than bending over and drinking it straight from the river.

General: I don't get it. Are we going to be fighting a war or having the Midianites over for cake and ice cream? I've always believed in having good table manners, but I wouldn't put it above good sword fighting.

Gideon: An experienced soldier would never bend all the way down. Otherwise, the enemy could sneak up on him. Only the best soldiers know to bring the water up to their mouths.

General: So the three hundred men we have left are the smartest and best soldiers we have.

Gideon: Exactly.

GIDEON BLOWS HIS HORN
Judges 7:9-8:35

Narrator: Gideon and his three hundred men prepared for battle with the Midianites. The camp was below them.

Gideon: Oh, golly, golly, golly. I am so nervous. This is the biggest gig I've ever played. Thousands of Midianites waiting for me to begin. This is going to be a tough crowd.

Soldier 1: Gideon, our band is warming up. We're just about ready.

Soldier 2: How do you like our sign?

Gideon: The Jerubbaal Jamboree Jazz Band. I don't think we want signs. This is supposed to be a surprise concert.

Soldier 1: When do we go on?

Gideon: As soon as we get a signal from the Great Conductor.

God: Gideon!

Gideon: Three hundred men against an entire army. It makes me real edgy. And I have heard that the Midianites are not a very good audience.

God: If you are nervous about attacking the Midianites, why don't you and your attendant Purah sneak into the camp and listen to them? That will give you courage.

Purah: Gideon, are you sure that you want to go out into that Midianite crowd?

Gideon: It's important to get the mood of the audience before we perform, Purah.

Purah: As you wish. You're the boss.

Midianite 1: Tickets, please.

Purah: Uh, we forgot them.

Midianite 2: You have to have tickets to get in. I'm calling the security guards.

Gideon: What's the big deal? Since when does a Midianite get so jittery that you have to call for security?

Midianite 1: Haven't you heard? Gideon and the Israelite band are on their way. We can't be too careful.

Purah: But you . . . er, I mean, we and our allies . . . are as thick as locusts and our camels are as numerous as the sands on the shore.

Midianite 2: That may be true. But my friend was telling me about a dream he had. In it a loaf of barley bread came whizzing into the Midianite camp and struck a tent. The tent fell down and turned over.

Gideon: A flying loaf of bread?

Midianite 1: Right. And everyone thinks the dream means that the bread is Gideon's sword and that the God of Israel will defeat us.

Gideon: Tell the boys to strike up the band. It's almost showtime!

Narrator: Gideon returned to the camp of Israel and shouted, "Come on! The Lord has delivered the Midianite camp into your hands."

Gideon: I'm dividing you into three groups. Stage right, stage left, and center stage. Is the ram's horn section ready?

Purah: Toot toot. And the special effects boys have given everyone empty jars with a torch inside.

Gideon: When I strike the first note, everyone begin playing and do your thing. Gentlemen, let's make music.

Announcer: Jerry Abiezer reporting live from the suprise concert of Gideon and his three hundred man band. The Midianite audience is seated . . . not at all aware of what is about to happen. This is *the* event of the decade. I am breathless.

Assistant: What a moment. Gideon is raising his horn. The band is waiting for his signal. Silence. There it is. The first note of Gideon's horn. Now, all the horns of the Israelites are joining in.

Announcer: Check out the special effects. Jars are being smashed everywhere and torches are being lit. The music, the sound, the lights. What a spectacular program.

Assistant: The Midianites are totally suprised. They're attacking each other in the darkness. Where is crowd control? The mob is in a frenzy. Midianites are going whacko.

Announcer: Yes, it is a new sound, but who could imagine the effect on the audience? Wow. Here come the tribes of Naphtali and Asher to chase after the Midianites who are running away.

Assistant: Bravo, bravo. This is perhaps the greatest concert in recorded history. Let's go backstage to help Gideon celebrate his Victory Tour.

Soldier: Gideon, there are some angry musicians here to see you from the tribe of Ephraim.

Ephraim 1: We found some of the Midianites that got away, including General Oreb and General Zeeb.

Gideon: Where are they?

Ephraim 2: Let's say that the concert really slayed them.

Gideon: So! What's the matter?

Ephraim 1: Why didn't you invite us to be in your band to suprise the Midianites? We have some pretty good players.

Gideon: So I see. Well, look at it this way, we played to the common Midianites, but you ended up playing for the head honchos. Tribe of Ephraim, you were great.

Ephraim 2: We were, weren't we?

Gideon: Thanks for all your help. Let's do lunch soon.

Narrator: Then Gideon took his men and came to the river Jordan and crossed it. The kings of Midian were fleeing with their armies and the Israelites were in pursuit.

Soldier: We've captured King Zebah and Zalmunna. What do you want us to do with them?

Gideon: So, you didn't like our show? It's very rude to walk out on a performance. It really upsets the musicians.

Zebah: Spare us. Our chariots were double parked. We're big fans of your band, really.

Gideon: Let me tell you a story. Remember those people that you killed at Tabor?

Zebah: Yes, they looked just like you.

Zalmunna: Great. First you come up with a silly excuse for leaving the show and then you admit to killing his family.

Gideon: Gentlemen, you will now face the ultimate ending.

Zalmunna: No. Please don't tear up our Gideon Fan Club Membership cards.

Narrator: And Gideon killed Zebah and Zalmunna and he took the crescents that were on the necks of their camels.

Soldier: Be our king. All of Israel wants you to rule us.

Purah: Please, Gideon, do as the people want.

Gideon: I will not be king. It's not right. But I will accept gifts as a reward for my performance.

Narrator: And each Israelite gave Gideon a piece of gold jewelry that had been taken as booty.

Gideon: I may be humble, but I'm not stupid. I can't go on playing concert halls forever.

Narrator: And Jerubbaal returned home and had seventy sons and lived to a ripe old age. Midian submitted to Israel and the land was at peace. But when Gideon died, the Israelites once again turned to idols and were disloyal to God.

JEPHTHAH AND HIS DAUGHTER
Judges 11:1-12:7

Narrator: Time passes, but old habits continue. The Israelites forget God and copy the ways of their neighbors. They worship idols and God punishes them . . . and they repent.

Israelites: Woe to us. Woe to us. We been bad.

Narrator: Then God hears the prayers of the people and sends them a leader to help them defeat their enemies. When the crisis is over, the Israelites once again start praying to idols. And God punishes them . . . and they . . .

Israelites: Woe to us, woe to us. We been bad.

Narrator: And so it goes.

Israelite 1: Woe to us. The Ammonites are attacking and there is no leader to defend us.

Israelite 2: There's gotta be someone. How about Dan the shepherd?

Israelite 3: Are you kidding? His sheep don't even listen to him.

Israelite 1: What about Avram the potter?

Israelite 3: The one who makes the five legged ceramic camels? Not a good choice. But who?

Israelite 2: I hate to say it, but there's one man who hasn't been mentioned. What about Jephthah?

Israelite 1: He's a scoundrel, a pirate, and you know about his past.

Israelite 2: Shhh. There might be children around.

Israelite 3: He was kicked out of his family's estate by his half brothers because he's a son of a . . .

Israelite 2: Shhh. Let's not gossip . . . even though we all know it's true.

Israelite 3: Jephthah is a rogue.

Israelite 1: He surrounds himself with thieves and criminals.

Israelite 2: Let's face it. He's perfect for the job.

Narrator: And the elders of Gilead went to get Jephthah.

Elder 1: Jephthah, our brother and friend.

Jephthah: Excuse me. Are you talking to me? The kid voted "Most likely to be hated"?

Elder 2: Jephthah, the Ammonites have attacked Israel and we need a strong leader.

Jepthah: So that's what this is all about. I get no respect. First you kick me out of town. You drive me from my father's home. And now, you want me to fight the Ammonites for you?

Elder 3: So call us fickle. We're sorry. But look at it this way. If you defeat the Ammonites, you get to boss us all around.

Jephthah: Oooh. This I like!

Elder 1: The Lord is a witness between us. We will do just as you say.

Jephthah: Where do I sign?

Narrator: Jephthah went with the elders of Gilead and the people made him their commander and chief. And Jephthah repeated all these terms before the Lord at Mitzpah.

Messenger: Jephthah, I have returned with an answer from the Ammonite king.

Jepthah: What did he say when I asked him why he chose to make war on Israel?

Messenger: Well, it was kind of a long answer. But the Ammonites want the land that Israel took from them three hundred years ago.

Jephthah: Three hundred years ago? Why didn't they do anything about it then? Is this king playing with a full deck?

Narrator: And the spirit of God came upon Jephthah and he marched against the Ammonites.

Jephthah: God, before all these elders of Israel I make a vow and I will keep it if You help me defeat the Ammonites.

Elder 1: God isn't asking for anything. Don't make a vow, Jephthah.

Jephthah: If I win, I'll give You my favorite robe.

Elder 2: I don't think God needs a robe, Jephthah.

Jephthah: All right. I'll tell you what. If I win this war against the Ammonites, I will give You whatever comes out of my house first upon my safe return.

Narrator: And Jephthah crossed over to the Ammonites and attacked them. And the Lord delivered the Ammonites into his hands and the Ammonites surrendered.

Jephthah: This is wonderful. I have defeated the Ammonites and now I am the leader of the Israelites. What could be better? Ahh . . . home sweet home.

Daughter: Father, congratulations. Welcome home, I'm so glad to see you.

Jephthah: Get back in the house.

Daughter: Well, I'm glad you're so happy to see me, too. What am I, chopped liver?

Jephthah: That about sums it up. I promised God the first thing that came out of my house if I was victorious.

Daughter: Oops. Maybe, I'll go back inside the house and send out the goat.

Jephthah: It's too late.

Daughter: You couldn't promise God something simple. You had to be creative.

Jephthah: It seemed like a good idea at the time. I should have just stuck with pledging my favorite robe.

Daughter: But instead you offered your favorite and only child. Well, a vow is a vow. Give me two months to prepare for my fate.

Jephthah: What will you do?

Daughter: I will take some of my friends up into the hills and think for a while about my life. And then I'm going to have a nice long cry. A very long cry.

Narrator: And Jephthah's daughter and companions went away for two months. Upon her return, she went to her father and was never seen again. And so began a custom that, every year for four days, the maidens of Israel would go and have a good cry for the daughter of Jephthah. And Jephthah led the Israelites for six years.

59

SAMSON: THE EARLY YEARS
Judges 13:1-15:20

Raphael: Ladies and gentlemen. Welcome to "This is Your Life." The exciting talk show that is sweeping the Land of Israel. My name is Raphael and I'm the host with the most surprises. Tonight, we'll be suprising the man who has been the chief judge of the Israelites for the past twenty years — Samson. He's hip, he's strong, he's got hair down to here. Do you love a surprise? Oh, I adore surprises. Let's go suprise him. He's down in our sound studio right now filming a public service announcement.

Director: Quiet on the set.

Samson: How's my hair look?

Assistant: Fabulous. All those curls are going to just shimmer in the light.

Director: Okay. Action.

Samson: Hello, Israel. Are you tired of being bullied by the Philistine punks in the neighborhood? Tired of being pushed around by . . . Raphael, what are you doing here?

Raphael: Samson, now relax and stay calm. Remember your temper and keep those biceps unflexed. You're going to love this.

Samson: Raphael, I don't have time right now. I'm doing a public service announcement and I don't want to be disturbed.

Raphael: Samson the Judge — THIS IS YOUR LIFE.

Director: Could someone please get Raphael some water? I think Samson knocked him out.

Samson: I hate surprises. I hate surprises.

Assistant: Samson, save that macho stuff for the Philistines. Give the poor fellow a break.

Samson: I just did.

Assistant: He's just doing his job. Besides, your public deserves to know the real you.

Samson: All right, all right. Bring on the guests.

Manoah: (from offstage) We had no children and had just about given up hope on having any when an angel of the Lord appeared to us and told us we would have a son.

Mother: (from offstage) But we had to promise that the boy would serve God. So, I couldn't have any liquor while I was pregnant and we took a vow that our son would be a Nazirite. No haircuts and he can't have liquor.

Samson: I give up. Who are they?

Raphael: Your parents. Mr. and Mrs. Manoah from the tribe of Dan.

Samson: I would have never guessed.

Wife: (from offstage) I was Samson's first love. Even though he was an Israelite and I was a Philistine, we kind of dug each other.

Manoah: I won't be seen on the stage with that Philistine woman.

Samson: Who? Who is it? Have you guessed who it is, Dad?

Raphael: Samson, it's your first wife. You fell in love with her and had your parents arrange a marriage.

Samson: I remember her. It's all coming back to me.

Lion: (from offstage) Roar. What a totally embarrassing

experience. I was supposed to be the king of the jungle. I see this guy coming along and he looks like a tasty snack. Instead, he tears me apart with his bare hands. This guy is tough.

Samson: It's the lion. I got it, right? How're you doing?

Lion: Stay away from me. You're dangerous.

Philistine: (from offstage) "Out of the eater came something to eat; Out of the strong came something sweet." That's the riddle you bet nobody could solve during the wedding feast. And we couldn't until we talked your wife into getting the answer out of you. Remember the dumb look on your face when we gave you the right response?

Samson: It's the little Philistine runt that cheated me out of my bet and then ran off with my wife. Let me get my hands on him.

Raphael: Samson, calm down. He's gone. What we in the audience want to know is the answer to that riddle.

Samson: I went back to see the lion's skeleton and bees had built a hive. Get it? The lion was strong and the honey was sweet.

Lion: You mean they built a honey bee hive on my grave. This is even more embarrassing. Can't a lion lie in peace? Are we still on the air? I hope my family isn't watching.

Raphael: Do you hate the Philistines because they cheated on the riddle?

Samson: That, and the fact that one of them ran off with my wife. Besides, they've been pushing the Israelites around for a long time. I don't know. Maybe I'm just a little too sensitive.

Raphael: Yes, but most men wouldn't get even by setting fire to their fields and vineyards and then killing one thousand Philistines with the jawbone of a donkey.

Samson: Sure they would. Besides, what I did to the Philistines couldn't have happened to a more rotten group of people.

Raphael: Remind me not to get you angry at me again.

Lion: Count me in on that.

Raphael: Samson, we're almost out of time. I know that you have a busy schedule fighting the Philistines with your incredible strength. Where does it come from?

Samson: Do magicians tell you how they do their tricks? Do teachers tell you how they seem always to know the exact moment to turn around and catch you in the act? I'm a professional.

Raphael: There you have it. Samson — judge over Israel for twenty years — THIS IS YOUR LIFE.

SAMSON AND DELILAH
Judges 16:1-16:31

Man: Step right in, gentlemen. We have a great show for you and it starts in just three minutes. There are no prettier ladies than here at the Gaza Strip.

Samson: How much?

Man: Twenty shekels. Hey, aren't you Samson?

Samson: How did you know that?

Man: They're aren't many people with thirty inch biceps and hair down to the floor who would dare wear a T-shirt in Philistine country that says "I use Philistines for toothpicks."

Samson: You flatter me.

Man: Tell ya what . . . you can go in for free, as long as you promise not to lose your temper and tear the place apart.

Samson: Why would I do that?

Man: Rumor has it that the last joint you visited, you got annoyed because the doorway was too narrow. So you took the entire door with the gateposts and the bar and moved it out of the way.

Samson: Doors can be such an inconvenience.

Delilah: Hi, there, big boy. I'm Delilah. Do you come here often? What's your name?

Samson: Call me Samson. . . . and, I think I'm in love.

Delilah: Well, Samson, it's a pleasure to meet you. Is that hair all yours? You could shelter a flock of birds in there.

Narrator: So Samson fell in love with a woman from the

Wadi Sorek named Delilah. Afterward, the lords of the Philistines came to her.

Philistine 1: Delilah, it's your patriotic duty to find out what makes your boyfriend Samson so strong. The Philistines are depending on you.

Delilah: Spare me all that patriotism.

Philistine 2: We'll each pay you eleven hundred shekels of silver.

Delilah: How's that Philistine national anthem go again?

Philistine 1: Remember, we'll be right outside waiting to overpower him once we know the secret of his strength.

Delilah: You've got a deal. Everybody out. Here comes my boyfriend.

Samson: Delilah, my love, let's party.

Delilah: Samson, answer me this first. What makes you so strong? What would make you helpless? Please tell me. Kissy kissy.

Samson: All right. If you tie me up with seven tendons, I'll become as weak as an ordinary man.

Delilah: Here are seven tendons. There now, you're all tied up. Uh oh, here come the Philistines.

Samson: I'll annihilate them.

Delilah: You broke out of the tendons. You lied to me, Samson. Oh pooh.

Samson: Delilah, it was a joke. If I told you the secret of my strength, it would take the mystery out of our relationship.

Philistine 1: Psst. Hey, girlie. We promised you a lot of shekels and all you do is play weird games. Get with the program.

Philistine 2: This is serious. You've tied him up with tendons, then new rope, and then even a web made up of hair from his head.

Delilah: He likes playing games.

Philistine 2: You're trying to use your womanly charms to find out the source of his strength. How about a new approach?

Delilah: So, how do you suggest I get the answer out of him?

Philistine 2: Nag him. Go to it and we'll be waiting.

Delilah: Samson, please, please, please. You don't love me. Please, please. I have to know. It's not fair. I thought you said you liked me.

Samson: Delilah, you have been at this for hours. If it's that important to you, I'll tell you. After all, I love you.

Delilah: And I love you.

Samson: I am a Nazirite and my hair has never been cut. If it was, I'd become as weak as an ordinary man. That's the truth.

Delilah: Thanks, sucker.

Samson: What?

Delilah: Supper. I'll get supper. You take a nap. Night, night. Good boy. Now, for dinner, here's some lambchops and a crew cut. The Philistines are upon you. Wake up.

Philistine 2: Grab him. He's no longer strong.

Samson: How could you do this to me?

Delilah: Each one of these guys gave me eleven hundred shekels.

Samson: Good answer.

Narrator: The Philistines seized Samson and gouged out his eyes. They brought him down to Gaza and put him in chains.

King: Devoted Philistines. Today is a great day, for our god has delivered Samson into our hands. So come on over to the temple because I'm throwing a major blowout of a party.

Courtesan: Highness, this is going great. Everyone is here. Three thousand party animals under one roof. And we have a special treat for the crowd.

M.C.: Settle down, everyone. We are proud to open tonight's show with a terrific number. You have all feared him. He has burned our fields, killed our soldiers, and been downright annoying. You know him as Samson.

All: Boo.

M.C.: Tonight Samson will dance before us. Don't let his blindness fool you. He was clumsier when he could see. But, seriously, folks, here he is, our number one enemy, Samson the slave.

All: Boo.

Boy: You're on, Mr. Samson.

Samson: Sounds like a tough crowd.

Boy: Three thousand people and they all hate you.

Samson: Keep building up my ego, kid. After I dance, lead me to the pillars that hold up this temple.

Narrator: Samson was fetched from prison and danced for the Philistines. Then they put him between the pillars.

Samson: God, please remember me and give me the strength just this once to take revenge on the Philistines.

Boy: Look, Samson is embracing the pillars and is pushing against them.

Samson: Hey, Philistines, how'd you like the show?

All: Boo.

Samson: I thought my dancing was great. In fact, let's just say my performance is going to bring the house down. But there will be no encore.

Narrator: Samson pushed with all his might and the temple came crashing down on the Philistine lords and all the people, too. And Samson also died. And his family carried him up and buried him in the tomb of his father. He had led Israel for twenty years.

DAN FINDS A HOME

Judges 17:1-18:31

Announcer: Welcome to another episode of Negev Valley Days. Each week, we look at a different story about the old Israelite country and how it was won. Now this here tale takes place way back in the time of judges before they had kings. Folks did just as they pleased. If you look at a map from the old days, you'll notice that the tribe of Dan had land in the south as well as land way up north. How'd that happen? Well pardners, sit back a spell and I'll tell ya.

Voice: This portion sponsored by Club Camel — the affordable vacation for the young and adventurous.

Announcer: It all got started with this feller named Micah who was out lookin' for someone to be his priest on account of his wantin' to build himself his own personal temple.

Micah: Woe, horsey. Slow down. Hey mister. Watcha doin' in these parts? Don'tcha know a feller can get hurt hitchhikin' around the hills of Ephraim? We still got Philistine raiders and thieves here.

Levite: Don't got much choice. I lost my horse.

Micah: You're not from around these here parts. Where do you hail from?

Levite: I'm a Levite from Bethlehem in Judah, but I'm a travelin' man. I go where my feet take me. And right now, they're not takin' me anywhere.

Micah: Hot doggy. I need a Levite. I just built me a house of God and I need a priest. My old lady gave me eleven hundred shekels and I got me this fancy silver molten image. Be my priest.

Levite: I don't know. I like the open road.

Micah: Ten shekels a year and all expenses paid.

Levite: Well, it's a chance to rest my tired feet.

Announcer: Meanwhile, down south, the people of the tribe of Dan were surrounded by hostile Philistines and getting pushed around right badly. They were in heaps of trouble.

Danite 1: Boys, we need to send out a scouting party and find us a new piece of land before the Philistines attack. They could make Custer's Last Stand look like a tea party. The tribe of Dan needs to move.

Danite 2: We'll send out five spies. They'll look for new territory where we can settle and homestead.

Voice: We'll return to our story in a moment. Club Camel. Ten days in Damascus or a week-long cruise down the Nile will make you feel human again. Drop your shepherd's hook, your farming tools, your fishing nets, and come away to Club Camel. Kosher accommodations all the way.

Announcer: So the Danites set out to scout the land and came upon the territory near Micah's home.

Spy 1: Check out the bright lights coming from the saloon.

Spy 2: What do the light's say?

Spy 1: Micah's Motel and Mission.

Levite: Howdy, strangers. What are you dudes up to?

Spy 1: We're scoutin' out the land to settle part of the tribe of Dan. What about you? You're a Levite, aren't you?

Levite: Sure enough. My boss, Micah, hired me to be his priest and watch over his temple.

Spy 2: Levite, will we be successful in scouting out new territory?

Levite: I reckon you will. Go in peace.

Announcer: And sure enough, the Danites found a place up north called Laish, which had been settled by nice folks. The spies went home and told their tribe the good news. Everybody was happy, except maybe the folks in Laish.

Spy 1: Hey, fellow Danites. Up north the land is good for farming and the people there won't give us much of a fight. Let's dust off the wagons and hit the trail.

Danite 1: Gather up six hundred warriors. Then round up the women and children and get the wagons rolling.

Danite 2: Wagons ho! I always wanted to say that.

Announcer: Now the Danite folks were passing through the hill country of Ephraim and the spies remembered the house of Micah. They told their chiefs about the Levite and the gold and silver ornaments in Micah's temple.

Danite 2: Wagons halt.

Danite 3: Knock knock.

Levite: We're closed.

Danite 4: Now you're open.

Levite: Who says so?

Danite 4: Me and the six hundred warriors standing outside the tent.

Levite: Coffee or tea for you gentlemen?

Danite 3: We need a priest where we're goin' and we figured that you might want to saddle up.

Levite: I'm mighty pleased that you want me to be your priest. Is it because of my incredible ability to work with folks and predict the future?

Danite 3: Uh . . . sure. Not to mention that you have a mighty impressive silver molten image and a lot of silver and gold ornaments that we will need for prayer when we get settled up north.

Levite: I guess you love me for my gold pots. When Micah finds out that I left with his treasures, he'll have me shot.

Danite 4: Be our priest. Why work for one man when you can be in charge of a whole tribe? Choose now, pardner. Whole tribe of Dan or one measly Micah?

Levite: I'll grab my gear.

Announcer: So the Levite took the sculptured images and he joined up with the wagon trail. When Micah returned, he was hotter than the sands of Sinai. He rustled up a posse to give chase. Before long, he caught up with the Danites.

Danite 1: Circle the wagons. Company's coming.

Micah: Hey, pardners, what have you done with my gold and silver? And it looks like you made off with my priest as well. I've got a lot of men here and we want some answers.

Danite 2: And we have six hundred warriors who have been without land for quite a spell. We're hot, we're hungry, we're angry, and we're fightin' mad.

Micah: Six hundred warriors? Hmmm . . .

Announcer: Micah realized that in a battle, he'd lose. So he turned hide and skiddadled. The wagon train continued northward and finally arrived in Laish, which they easily captured.

Levite: Okay, easy with the statues. Watch out for the molten image. Unload those wagons. Bring out the tools. We've got a town to build. Easy with the neon lights! Don't wrinkle the Elvis costume — I have a wedding to do tomorrow.

Announcer: The folks renamed the town Dan. Not a very creative bunch, but nobody minded. And that's how part of the tribe of Dan ended up in the north while the rest of the tribe stayed in the south. Happy trails, pardner.

SAMUEL IS BORN
I Samuel 1:1-2:21

Narrator: In the hill country of Ephraim, there lived a man by the name of Elkanah. He had two wives, Hannah and Peninah. This is their story.

Elkanah: I'm getting ready to go up to Shiloh to offer sacrifices to Adonai. Who wants to come with me?

Peninah: I don't know, Elkanah. With so many children to watch over it's hard to get away. Maybe Hannah will go. Since she has yet to give birth to a child, she has plenty of time for touring.

Hannah: I want children very badly. It's not my fault that I don't have any.

Peninah: Of course it isn't. I know three or four other women who don't have children.

Hannah: Really?

Peninah: Sure. But then again, they're not married either.

Hannah: Stop teasing me, Peninah. You do this all the time. Why?

Peninah: Because you're my rival and I hate you.

Hannah: That's reasonable.

Elkanah: Everybody is coming to Shiloh for the sacrifices. No discussion.

Peninah: Elkanah, why don't you ride with six or seven of our children? I'll carry the baby and, Hannah, you can carry the luggage.

Elkanah: Hannah, why are you crying? Don't you know that even if you don't have children, I love you.

Peninah: I heard that.

Elkanah: Well, here we are at the Shiloh temple. Anyone want something to eat?

Hannah: I'm not hungry. I'm still upset. I'm going inside to pray.

Narrator: Hannah rose and went into the temple of the Lord. Eli the Priest was sitting on a seat near the doorpost of the temple.

Hannah: (softly) Dear God, please let me have children. I can't stand not being a mother. Besides, Peninah is driving me crazy. I'll give You my first son. He'll serve you and no razor shall touch his head. Please help me.

Eli: Young lady, you should be ashamed of yourself. Carrying on like this in a temple. Shameful the way you young people drink these days.

Hannah: I am not drunk. I was praying to God for a child. My husband's other wife has many.

Eli: That wouldn't be the lady out there with the T-shirt that reads "Peninah 6 - Hannah 0."

Hannah: One and the same.

Eli: Go in peace. The Lord will grant you your wish.

Hannah: Oooh. Suddenly my appetite is back.

Narrator: Hannah conceived and bore a son. She named him Samuel, meaning, "I asked God for him."

Peninah: Luck, it was pure luck.

Elkanah: It is time to return to Shiloh to sacrifice to the Lord.

Hannah: Elkanah, I want to stay home with Samuel because when he is older, we must give him to God.

Peninah: Fine, there will be more food for the rest of us.

Narrator: And when Samuel was still very young, Hannah brought the boy to Eli.

Hannah: Eli, here is my son Samuel. It is the child I prayed for. I now give him to you. He is to serve God in this place for as long as you live.

Eli: Well, I can always use the help. You probably know that my sons are not exactly very helpful.

Hannah: I know them to be cheaters, liars, and scoundrels who abuse their rights as priests.

Eli: Those are my boys. The Israelite Mafia.

Hannah: Samuel, you're going to stay with Eli the Priest and serve God. Mommy will come visit you all the time. Make your momma proud.

Narrator: And God took note of Hannah and she bore three more sons and two daughters. Young Samuel, meanwhile, grew up in the service of God.

Hannah: Tie score, Peninah.

SAMUEL HEARS GOD

I Samuel 2:22-3:21

Eli: All right, Samuel, I'm going to bed now. Be sure not to stay up too late.

Samuel: I'm going to sleep, too, Eli. It's been quite a day taking care of the sanctuary.

Eli: Didn't my sons Hophni and Phinehas help out?

Samuel: They said they had a few parties to go to.

Eli: My little angels.

Samuel: They don't seem to take their job as priests very seriously.

Eli: What makes you say that?

Samuel: They spend a lot of time with the ladies. They cheat people out of their sacrifices. They trick people into giving more money to the temple, and then they keep it.

Eli: All right. All right. I am very old, but I am not senile. A messenger from God has already told me that I will be punished for having raised such bad sons. They will not lead the Israelites.

Samuel: Well, on that cheery note, good night, Eli.

Narrator: Now in those days the word of God was rare, prophesy was not widespread. Samuel was sleeping in the priestly tent where the Ark of God was kept.

God: Samuel.

Samuel: Eli, you called me. What do you want?

Eli: You must have been dreaming. Go back to sleep.

God: Samuel.

Samuel: Here we go again. Eli, you called me from your room. What do you want?

Eli: Oy. Again with the interruptions. I want you to leave me alone.

Samuel: But you called my name.

Eli: You must have been dreaming. Go back to sleep.

Samuel: Right – see you in the morning.

God: Samuel.

Samuel: Three times in a row. Eli must be going bonkers and just not know it. Eli, you called me. You said,"Samuel."

Eli: What are you talking about? I am not calling you.

Samuel: Somebody is.

Eli: Ridiculous. The only people in this place are the two of us. I'm alone in here and you're out there with the Ark. That's it. So, the next time you hear your name – don't wake me up. Just say, "Speak, for your servant is listening."

God: Samuel.

Samuel: Speak, for your servant is listening.

God: I am the God of Israel.

Samuel: Finally, I get to talk to someone.

God: Because Eli knew of the evil deeds of his sons and did not rebuke them, I will punish his house. There is nothing that can be done to prevent it.

Samuel: This is heavy stuff.

Eli: Good morning, Samuel. Did you speak with God last night?

Samuel: Kind of.

Eli: What did he say to you?

Samuel: Nothing much. Just chit chat. You know. How are you? Are you from Ramah? I know some people from that town. Stuff like that.

Eli: The truth, Samuel. I can handle it. God doesn't chit chat. If you don't tell me, may everything that God said would happen to me, happen to you double.

Samuel: Okay, here's the scoop. God says that your family is history. Your kids are bums, trash, scum of the earth, and more. You were a lousy dad for letting your kids get away with it. You will have no place in the leadership of Israel. Your entire house will be punished for their crimes.

Eli: Please . . . Don't hold back. How about the good news?

Samuel: I'm done. That's all there was. I'm real sorry, Eli.

Eli: God does what is best.

Narrator: Samuel grew up and God was with Him. All Israel, from Dan to Beersheva, knew that Samuel was a trustworthy prophet of God.

THE ARK IS CAPTURED
I Samuel 4:1-5:22

Servant: Soldiers are coming.

Phinehas: Excellent. I'm sure the news from the battlefield will be good.

Hophni: Which means there will be lots of victory sacrifices, by the people and that means, we get . . .

Both: Money!

Hophni: And even if Israel is defeated by the Philistines, then people will come to Shiloh to offer guilt sacrifices, which means we get . . .

Both: Money!

Phinehas: Gosh, I love being a priest.

Servant: Is that all you care about? Making money off of the people? What about spiritual guidance? What about helping others? You're the sons of Eli the Priest. What kind of priests are you?

Hophni: Evil, but rich.

Soldier: Phinehas and Hophni, the Philistines have killed four thousand of our men. We need you on the battlefield. The elders have asked you to bring the Ark of the Covenant.

Phinehas: That's risky. I'm sure it would help the morale among the troops, but Shiloh's entire tourist trade depends upon the Ark being here. The financial implications are vast.

Hophni: Besides, you would be putting your beloved priests in danger.

Servant: But think what it would do for business if you guys take the Ark into battle and win the day. Tourist trade will double.

Phinehas: Okay, boys, grab that Ark and let's hit the road.

Narrator: When the Ark of the Covenant entered the camp, all Israel burst into a great shout.

Israelites: One, two, hip hooray, the Ark of the Covenant will save the day!

Narrator: And the Philistines learned that the Ark of the Covenant had come to the camp and they were frightened.

Philistines: Oh no, woe, woe, we're bummed out, darn it.

Narrator: Philistines were not known for rhyming their poems.

Philistine: So what, the Ark of the Covenant is in their camp. Big deal. It's only the diety who struck the Egyptians with plagues and split the sea. Are we mice or men?

Philistines: Squeek, squeek.

Philistine: Be brave. If we lose, we'll become slaves to the Hebrews. We'll be doing their laundry. But, how can we lose? Look at the clowns that are leading them — two priests with coin changers on their belts. Attack!

Narrator: And the Philistines fought and defeated Israel. Thirty thousand Israelite soldiers fell that day.

Benjaminite: Eli, where is Eli?

Servant: What is it, young Benjaminite?

Benjaminite: I have bad news from the battlefield.

Servant: Okay, but be tactful. Eli is ninety-eight years old.

You must be careful in phrasing your words. He has been sitting beside the road waiting to hear news about the Ark of God.

Benjaminite: No problem.

Eli: What is the noise coming up from the town? It sounds like something has gone wrong.

Benjaminite: I come from the battlefield. I have some good news and some bad news. Which do you want first?

Servant: Careful.

Eli: I'll take the bad news.

Benjaminite: The Philistines defeated the Israelites in a great slaughter. Your sons were both killed and the Ark of God has been captured.

Eli: No, it can't be. Ahhhhh!

Servant: Now, you see what you did. Eli has fallen backwards off his chair. The news was too much for him.

Benjaminite: I guess that wasn't tactful enough. Should I give him a few moments to recover?

Servant: Take all the time you want. He has broken his neck and died. What was the good news?

Benjaminite: The wife of Phineas has given birth to a baby boy. Eli was a grandpa. She's named him Ichabod, meaning "Glory has departed from Israel."

Servant: Oh, that's cheerful.

THE ARK RETURNS
I Samuel 5:1-7:17

Narrator: When the Philistines captured the Ark of God, they brought it to their city of Ashdod.

Priest 1: Put it in the temple of Dagon. Yes, right next to the idol of Dagon. This is going to make us the pride of all of the five Philistine cities.

Soldier: Are you sure you want the Ark of the Israelites in the temple? It's very powerful.

Priest 1: Nonsense. We captured it. Dagon is more powerful than the God of Israel. If he isn't, I'll eat my hat.

Servant: Great priest, come quick. Dagon was found this morning face down on the ground in front of the Ark.

Soldier: I warned you.

Priest 1: Nonsense. The idol was probably loose. Set it back up. I told you. Dagon is more powerful than the God of Israel.

Servant: Great priest, come quick. Yesterday, we found Dagon fallen over. And today not only has he fallen over, but his head and both hands have been cut off.

Soldier: You were saying . . .

Servant: Not only that, but a great plague has struck the city.

Soldier: . . . something about if the God of Israel was more powerful than Dagon . . .

Priest 1: Give me my hat. Mmmm. Tastes great.

Soldier: What should we do?

Priest 1: I have an idea.

Priest 2: Greetings, great priest of Ashdod.

Priest 1: Have you come to admire the Ark?

Priest 2: Yes. Congratulations on being chosen to take care of it. I must admit that we in Gath are a bit jealous.

Priest 1: Well, we can't have that. We're the Philistines. A team. Share and share alike. What's ours is yours.

Soldier: Like the plague?

Priest 2: Huh?

Priest 1: He means like the praise one receives for having captured the Ark. We've had the honor long enough. Please remove the Ark and take it to Gath with you.

Priest 2: Thank you. The people of Gath have no idea what I bring them. They will be so suprised.

Soldier: That's an understatement.

Narrator: So they moved the Ark of God to Gath. And the plague broke out against the city, striking young and old alike.

Priest 3: Greetings, great priest of Gath.

Priest 2: Welcome, priest of Ekron. Have you come to admire the Ark? A bit envious? Well, we can't have that. We're all Philistines. What's ours is yours. Share and share alike. Please take the Ark to Ekron.

Priest 3: Your generosity is overwhelming. It must take a great man to be able to part with the Ark.

Priest 2: It's all in a day's work. Now, hurry up and take the Ark away before I change my mind.

Priest 3: The people of Ekron will be overjoyed. They'll be dancing in the streets.

Priest 2: Don't bet on it.

Narrator: And the Ark of God came to Ekron and the people cried out, "They moved the Ark of the God of Israel to Ekron to kill us. Send it away." There was the panic of death in the city.

Chief 1: I call this meeting of the Elders of the Philistines to order. Is there any new business?

Chief 2: Get the Ark of the Israelites out of my town. Let's give it to Gaza.

Chief 3: Thanks, but no thanks.

Chief 4: It's been seven months and that Ark has caused more trouble than it's worth.

Chief 1: I've asked some diviners and priests here to give us some advice.

Diviner: First of all, get rid of the Ark.

Chief 2: I second that. All in favor? It's unanimous.

Priest: Secondly, send it away with five golden stones and five golden mice, symbols of the plague and of the lords and people of the five Philistine cities.

Chief 3: This is getting expensive.

Diviner: You could always keep the Ark.

Chief 3: Expensive, but a worthwhile investment.

Priest: Put the Ark and the gold in a new cart that will be led by two cows. Then lead the cart to the border and let it go on its way.

Chief 4: I don't know. It seems like we're ending up the losers.

Diviner: You could harden your heart as Pharaoh did, and bring ten more plagues upon you and have your whole army drown. That certainly would make you popular with the people.

Narrator: So the Philistines led the cart as far as the border. And the cows took the road to Beth Shemesh. And the Philistines knew that it was truly the God of Israel that had sent the plague against them.

Israelite 1: Samuel, the Ark has been returned by the Philistines. It is now in Kiriath-Jearim being taken care of by Eleazar son of Abinadab.

Samuel: That's the sign I've been waiting for. Listen to me, people of Israel. Get rid of all the false idols in your homes. Serve only God and you will be delivered from the Philistines. Gather in Mizpah and we'll defeat them.

Narrator: When the Philistines heard that the Israelites were assembling at Mizpah, the lords of the Philistines marched against Israel.

Israelite 1: Samuel, what are we going to do? The Philistines are coming.

Samuel: That's usually what happens when there is a war. One side forms an army and then the other side's army comes to do battle.

Israelite 2: But they will destroy us as they always do.

Samuel: My, my. We certainly seem to have a lack of faith here. No need to worry. I have a strategy.

Israelite 3: What a relief. What is it? An ambush? A hit and run?

Samuel: Even better. I'm going to sacrifice this lamb to God.

Israelite 1: That's it. The Philistines are advancing and you're cooking.

Samuel: No problem. Where did I put my matches?

Israelite 2: Our soldiers are panicking. Look at the Philistines.

Samuel: God, save us from the hands of the Philistines.

Israelite 3: Listen to the thunder.

Samuel: That's what we call heavenly reinforcements.

Israelite 1: What do we do now?

Samuel: How about fighting back? An entirely new concept in dealing with the Philistines. Go knock a few heads together in the name of Israel.

Narrator: The men of Israel routed the Philistines and drove them back and humbled them. The Philistines did not invade the land of the Israelites again as long as Samuel lived. And Samuel led Israel, acting as its judge and seer.

ISRAEL WANTS A KING
I Samuel 8:1-21

Servant: Samuel, the elders of Israel are here to see you.

Samuel: But, I'm on vacation. They should know that when I'm in Ramah, it's for some R & R. Besides, I've appointed my sons to judge Israel.

Servant: They really want to see you. I think they want to discuss appointing a king.

Samuel: I told you not to say the "K" word in my presence.

Elder 1: Samuel, thank you for seeing us. We have an urgent matter to discuss.

Samuel: Why not talk to my sons? I've appointed them as judges.

Elder 2: Well, Joel and Abijah are, um, uh . . .

Samuel: Get to the point. I prefer that you be blunt.

Elder 3: They're bent on making a profit. They accept bribes. They subvert justice. They take from the rich and give to themselves. And they take from the poor and also give to themselves.

Elder 1: Let's face it, they're bums.

Samuel: Boys will be boys.

Elder 2: They're not kids. They're bums. Big bums, and you're no spring chicken anymore.

Samuel: You don't have to be that blunt. What would you have me do?

Elder 3: Appoint a king for us.

Servant: You shouldn't say the "K" word. Samuel doesn't like it.

Samuel: You have a king. God is your King.

Elder 1: But, we want a human king so that we can be like all the other nations.

Samuel: And if every other nation wore their shirts inside out, does that mean we should?

Elder 2: Please, we want to be like everyone else.

Samuel: Pushy people. Hold on a second, I must first consult with my Advisor.

God: You called?

Samuel: The people are kvetching again. They want a king. They want to be like every other nation. Is having a king going to be good or bad for the Jewish people?

God: Give them their king.

Samuel: I wish You hadn't said that! Oh, well . . .

God: Samuel, it is I that should be upset. They're not rejecting you. They're rejecting Me. But this has been going on since they left Egypt. Sometimes the best way to teach children is to give them what they want.

Samuel: Like letting them eat all the chocolate they want until they get a stomach ache.

God: But first, give them warning.

Samuel: I read You loud and clear. Over and out. Elders of Israel, I have spoken to God, and you shall have a king.

Elders: Hip hip hooray!

Samuel: But first, I must warn you.

Elders: Okay, but could you make it quick?

Samuel: The practice of a king is to take your sons away to be soldiers.

Elder 1: Check.

Samuel: You'll have to plow his fields and harvest his crops.

Elder 2: Check, we can handle it.

Samuel: He'll take your choice lands for himself and his court. He'll take your slaves for himself. You'll have to pay taxes.

Elder 3: Check. Is that all?

Samuel: He'll take your livestock. Your daughters will be taken to be bakers and cooks. The day will come when you will cry out and God will not answer you.

Elder 1: Check. But we still want to have a king. We want to be like everyone else.

Samuel: You are in for one big tummy ache. But, yes, I will appoint a king for you.

Elder 2: Great! When? Like, on what day?

Samuel: Go home. That day is coming.

THE FIRST KING OF ISRAEL
I Samuel 9:1-10:27

Narrator: There was a man of Benjamin named Kish. He had a son whose name was Saul.

Saul: I can't believe we lost all those donkeys. It's like they just disappeared.

Servant: C'mon Saul, let's go into Zuph. I hear there's a prophet there who knows everything. Donkey hunting is tough work. We need a break.

Saul: We really should be heading home. We have been looking for those lost donkeys of my father's all over the tribe of Benjamin. I'm pooped. Pop's gonna start worrying.

Servant: If we talk to the prophet, maybe he can tell us where you misplaced the donkeys.

Saul: Good idea. Let's ask those girls who are drawing water where he is. Ladies, is the man of God nearby?

Lady 1: Gosh, you sure are tall.

Lady 2: And awfully cute. You're blushing. Tell us what you want.

Saul: I want my donkeys.

Lady 1: Well, you certainly know how to ruin a romantic opportunity.

Lady 2: The man of God is straight ahead. He's blessing a sacrifice.

Saul: Hi there, priest. Can you tell me where the prophet is staying?

Samuel: Tah dah. You're looking at him . . . and I have been looking for you. Have a bite to eat, Saul. Relax for a while and spend the day. God has commanded me to speak to you.

Saul: Then God knows where my donkeys are?

Samuel: Forget the donkeys. They've already been found. I've been looking for you. All of Israel has been seeking you.

Saul: Why are you talking like this to me? I think I want to go home.

Samuel: I'm going to make known to you the word of God.

Saul: All I want to do is find my donkeys. I don't want to talk to God. I have nothing to say. I'm from a little clan in the smallest tribe of Israel.

Samuel: This is oil and I'm going to pour it on your head.

Saul: But I already use a conditioner.

Samuel: This is harder than I thought it would be. This is holy oil and with it I am anointing you to rule over God's people.

Saul: You've got to be kidding! Me, king of Israel?

Samuel: To prove to you that I'm serious, you will come across a number of signs on the way home. You'll meet three men on a pilgrimage and a band of prophets. You will pray with them. When you get back home, wait for me.

* * *

Uncle: Saul, where have you been?

Saul: Uncle, pinch me. I must have been dreaming. I dreamed that I met Samuel the prophet and then I fell in with this band of prophets for a while.

Uncle: But, it's true, you did speak to Samuel.

Saul: I was afraid you'd say that.

Narrator: But, Saul did not tell his uncle anything that Samuel had said about the kingship.

* * *

Announcer: Welcome to the "King of Israel Pageant," broadcasting live from Mizpah. All the tribes have been assembled and the crowd is eager to see who Samuel will crown as King of Israel.

Assistant: Insiders think it will be someone from one of the big tribes like Ephraim or Judah, but only Samuel knows.

Announcer: A hush has come over the people. The lots have been cast.

Samuel: The envelope, please. I ask that the tribe of Benjamin step forward.

Assistant: Did you hear the gasp from the crowd? Who'd have thought that it would be someone from the smallest tribe? The lots are now cast for the clan.

Samuel: The envelope. I call on the Matrite clan.

Announcer: Holy Moses. They're a teensy-weensy clan. What an upset!

Samuel: The first king of Israel, the man who you have chosen today over the God who delivered you out of Egypt and who you have constantly rejected, will be . . .

Announcer: Samuel certainly tells it like it is.

Samuel: Saul, son of Kish.

Assistant: Where is he? Show us our king.

Person: He's hiding among the baggage.

Announcer: Terrific, our first king is bashful. We're off to a great start!

All: Long live the king!

Samuel: Stop the shouting. I will now go over the rules of kingship.

Assistant: Not another speech about the evils of having a king.

Samuel: Okay, I'll just write the rules down in a book. You can all go home now. You must all be thrilled that you have a king at last.

Narrator: But some of the people were not happy. They scorned Saul and asked, "How can this fellow save us?"

SAUL'S FIRST BATTLE
I Samuel 11:1-14

M.C.: Welcome to "Biblical Melodrama." Tonight's presentation features King Saul, just recently crowned and feeling mighty spiffy.

All: Yeah. Hoorah.

M.C.: But hark, it's the evil Nahash the Ammonite who thinks that Saul will be a weak king. Does he think this just because Saul hid behind the baggage when he was chosen by Samuel to lead the nation?

All: Boo, hiss.

M.C.: We find Nahash and his band of miscellaneous villains surrounding the city of Jabesh-Gilead.

Nahash: You must give me the keys to your city.

Mayor: Let us make a pact — we will serve you and you will let us live.

Nahash: I'll make a pact with you, all right, but only if you agree that every person's right eye will be poked out.

Mayor: That's not reasonable.

Nahash: Of course not. I'm the bad guy. I am Nahash.

All: Boo, hiss.

Mayor: Give us seven days. If nobody comes to our aid, we'll surrender.

M.C.: So messengers came to King Saul and told him what was happening in Jabesh-Gilead.

Saul: Send out the word that we need soldiers to fight against the villain, Nahash.

Messenger: But what if the people are afraid to follow you?

Saul: Then tell them that every cow they own will be turned into hamburgers in the royal slaughterhouse.

Messenger: That's one message to go. Will that be all?

M.C.: Saul gathered a force of 330,000 soldiers in Bezek. They didn't want their cattle and oxen to end up at Ye Royal Burger Tent.

Nahash: It's been seven days. You must hand over the keys to the city.

Mayor: But, we can't hand over the keys to the city.

Nahash: But, you must hand over the keys to the city.

Mayor: But, we can't hand over the keys to the city.

Saul: I'll hand over the keys to the city.

All: Yeah, hooray.

Nahash: So, it's the little king who hides behind the baggage.

All: Boo, hiss.

Saul: Yes, evil Nahash. It is I, the little king, with 330,000 of my closest friends.

Nahash: Gulp.

Saul: Your manaical plan to create a chain of monocle stores is over.

All: Yeah, hooray.

Mayor: Oh, Saul, you've saved the day. Hardly an Ammonite is left. Our hero. Sigh, sigh.

Samuel: Let us go to Gilgal and officially inaugurate King Saul. And then we'll have a party.

Nahash: Curses, foiled again.

SAMUEL'S INAUGURATION ADDRESS
I Samuel 12:1-12:25

Israelite 1: I love your dress for the Inauguration Ball. What kind of material is that?

Israelite 2: It's a goatskin skirt with little furballs. It's the rage in Phoenicia.

Israelite 3: This is so exciting. Everyone . . . and I mean everyone . . . in Israel is here.

Israelite 1: Look at the program. The sacrifices of well-being are first.

Israelite 2: I always look forward to that.

Israelite 1: And the keynote speaker is Samuel the Prophet. Shhh. The ceremony is begining.

Host: Remember. You're supposed to loosen the crowd up.

Comedian: Relax. I'm a professional.

Host: You're on.

Comedian: Thank you, ladies and gentlemen. My job is to warm up the audience. Who wants to be the first sacrifice? Yuck, yuck. Moving right along, how about that Nahash guy who wanted to poke out the right eye of everyone in Jabash-Gilead? The way those guys drive camels up there, who'd of known the difference?

Host: Psst. Get off the stage. You're awful.

Comedian: Seriously, folks, I'd like to introduce a swell prophet who has been judging us wisely for a long time. You know him as Samuel. Thank you for being such a great audience.

Host: You'll never work in the Fertile Crescent again.

Samuel: You have asked me to set a king over you and I have done so. I'm old and gray and I've been your leader since my youth.

Israelite 1: Uh,oh. We're in for a long evening.

Samuel: And I have never once cheated you or taken a bribe.

Host: You have never taken anything from anyone.

Samuel: Then the Lord is witness to the fact that you have found nothing in my possession. Now, I shall tell you a story of our people. I've prepared a little slide presentation.

Israelite 2: Not the story about how we were slaves in Egypt!

Samuel: We were slaves in Egypt. May I have Egypt on the screen? There it is. What a tourist trap! Jacob took his sons down to Egypt and wasn't allowed to return for over four hundred years.

Comedian: Talk about tough customs procedures.

Samuel: Here's a slide of our ancestors leaving Egypt after crying out to God. Here they are entering the Promised Land.

Israelite 3: I think I see my great grandpa Murray.

Samuel: Here is Israel forgetting God and bowing to idols . . . Here they're being punished by falling into the hands of Sisera of Hazor . . . Then into the hands of the Philistines . . . and the Moabites . . . Oops, sorry, that's my son Joel at his sixth birthday party.

Israelite 1: The slides are in the right order. His sons should come right after the Moabites . . . the little monsters.

Samuel: This is a shot of Israel crying out that they sinned and . . . being saved by Gideon, Japhtheh, and me. Lights.

Israelite 2: Here comes the warning about having a king.

Samuel: But you wanted a king. You want to be like everyone else. Remember to obey the Lord. If you and your king follow God, good things will happen. Now, to prove my point. May I have a volunteer from the audience?

Israelite 3: Me? How exciting?

Samuel: What would be a good miracle this time of year?

Israelite 3: It's harvest time. How about thunder and rain?

Samuel: Thunder and rain for the lady and for all of Israel. Voila.

Israelite 2: God is so powerful. Maybe we shouldn't have a king.

Samuel: It's too late now. Just remember my message to you. It's not smart to fool with Adonai.

SAUL'S FIRST MISTAKE
I Samuel 13:1-14:52

Narrator: Saul ruled over Israel for two years. He kept 2,000 soldiers with him and 1,000 soldiers accompanied his son, Jonathan. Jonathan struck down the Philistine governor in Geba and the Philistines gathered to attack.

Saul: Okay, Israelites. We've got a great team here. I think we are going to take the Philistines.

Soldier 1: They beat us almost everytime we fight them.

Saul: But we have something that they don't have. We've got spirit.

Soldier 2: And they have something that we don't have — chariots, swords, and spears.

Saul: Coach Samuel will be here soon for the burnt offering.

Soldier 3: We've been waiting for him for seven days.

Soldier 2: And our loyal fans are hiding in caves and tunnels because they're so scared of what will happen if the Philistines win.

Saul: Where's your team spirit? Come on, how about a cheer?

Soldier 1: How about us going home? Let's forfeit.

Saul: Wait! I'll do the burnt offering myself and then we'll take the field.

Narrator: Saul had just finished presenting the burnt offering when Samuel arrived.

Saul: Greetings, Coach. I thought you'd never get here.

Samuel: What did you do?

Saul: Well, the team was bummed out and it looked like they would all quit, so I went ahead with the burnt offering. Did I do well?

Samuel: What kind of team captain are you? The Lord had commanded that you wait for me. You could have been team captain forever. You and your descendants could have been a dynasty. But no chance now.

Saul: Does this mean you won't renew my contract?

Samuel: The Owner has told me that I'm going to have to let you go. However, we're going to keep you around until a replacement can be found.

Saul: You won't be sorry.

Narrator: Jonathan and his attendant crossed over to the Philistine garrison and did battle against the enemy. Terror broke out in the Philistine camp and the very earth quaked.

Saul: All right, team. Let's bring the Ark of God up to center position. Everybody get ready to attack.

Soldier 1: It looks like the enemy is in total confusion. Would it be fair to attack before they're organized and ready?

Soldier 2: Fair? Which team has the swords and spears?

Saul: Before we charge up the field, I want you all to take a vow that nobody eats any food before nightfall when I take revenge on my enemies.

Soldier 3: This is the toughest spring training I've ever been to.

Saul: It's time for the kick off.

Narrator: Saul and his troops found the Philistines in great confusion. Thus God brought victory to Israel that day.

Saul: Let's go after the Philistines that got away.

Soldier 2: After we eat. I've never been so hungry. To have to pass by those honey bee hives was torture.

Saul: Now that you're fed, let's check with the Owner about finishing off the Philistines.

Priest: There's no answer. I've been trying for a while.

Saul: Something is wrong. The Owner's always answered before.

Priest: Maybe somebody broke the vow of eating and we're being punished.

Saul: I want to know now which guy broke training.

Jonathan: Hi, pops. What a victory!

Saul: You have honey dripping from your mouth.

Jonathan: Yeah, I scooped some out of the honey hive early this afternoon.

Saul: There was a vow made that nobody could eat today.

Jonathan: How was I supposed to know that? I was across the river fighting the Philistines.

Saul: As the God who brought victory to Israel lives, even though victory came through my son, Jonathan, he must be put to death because he broke the rules.

Soldier 2: This is one tough team captain.

Soldier 3: Saul, the troops can't let you put Jonathan to death. He brought us great victory.

Saul: What a team!

Narrator: And Saul broke off his pursuit of the Philistines that day. He waged war against the Moabites, Edomites, and the Philistines. And Saul and his wife, Ahinoam, had three sons, Jonathan, Ishvi, and Malchishua, and two daughters, Merab and Michal.

SAUL MAKES AN EVEN WORSE MISTAKE

I Samuel 15:1-35

Saul: It was a cool, dark day when the old man appeared in my office. He was like a man on fire, full of passion and pretty steamed up. How can I help you, Samuel, I said.

Samuel: The time has come to repay an old debt. God is commanding you to make a hit.

Saul: I looked in the old prophet's eyes and could see that he meant what he said. So I was finally getting another case.

Samuel: The nation of Amalek has to be pay for what it did to Israel on the road up from Egypt.

Saul: I nearly fell out of my chair. Amalek was one tough nation. Baddest of the bad. I had heard about the way they attacked Israel from behind because they knew that's where the old men and the children would be.

Samuel: Attack Amalek and destroy everything. Not a person or animal should be spared.

Saul: Holy moly. This was going to be a massacre. I took out my violin case. I knew I'd need a few of the boys to make this hit.

Slick: Hey, boss. I've rounded up the old gang to handle the job.

Saul: Slick was a friend, a pal, a kid of the streets, a wild dude, and yes, a fictional character.

Slick: Two hundred and ten thousand of the boys are ready to go. Let's do it.

105

Saul: We surrounded the main city and I told the peaceful Kenites living there to scoot, skedaddle, take a hike. They did. Charge, I said. Kings say that a lot.

Slick: Hey, boss. We smashed them. We've won a total victory. And look what we got.

Saul: Standing in front of me was King Agag — a man with a face that only a mother could love. He was cold as ice . . . he knew he might die. I toyed with his mind. King Agag, care for some tea?

Agag: Spare me the courtesy. You've killed everyone in my kingdom except me and my best sheep and oxen. Go ahead, finish me off.

Saul: I had to admire the guy. He was royal and tough — a streetwise king who rolled with the punches. One lump or two?

Samuel: There you are. I've been looking all over for you.

Saul: My heart was filled with pride as I greeted the old prophet. He had put his faith in me. I did a good job. The nation was bound to prosper. I looked forward to a night home with the doll.

Samuel: Why do I hear the sound of sheep and oxen?

Saul: Gulp, I said. The "bleat, bleat" gave me away.

Samuel: God commanded you to do away with every living creature among the Amalekites.

Saul: I had to think quick. My reputation was on the line. I blurted out the truth. Me and the boys spared the best of the animals to sacrifice to God.

Samuel: You disobeyed. God talked to me last night. You are finished. You'll never work this town again. The jig is up. Sure, you're still the head man, but you're on your way out.

We're all sorry you got the job. You were supposed to finish off the Amalek gang.

Agag: Saul, do you have any Sleepy Time tea?

Samuel: You spared King Agag and took spoils? That wasn't the deal. The Almighty doesn't want your sacrifices. God wants obedience.

Saul: I begged forgiveness. I wanted another chance. But the old guy just told me that the Almighty was rejecting me as king. I was history. The writing was on the wall. I was desperate, scared, frantic. I grabbed for his robe and it tore.

Slick: Boss, now you did it. First, you don't finish off the hit and now you tear the prophet's threads. This ain't your day.

Samuel: Bring me King Agag.

Agag: So, it's you, the old prophet . . . with the see-through robe.

Saul: Me and the boys just watched as the two toughs stood on disputed turf. You could hear a pin drop.

Agag: Bitter death is at hand.

Samuel: I'm glad we agree on something. Say goodnight, Agag.

Saul: The old guy cut down the king. It was a powerful moment. Then he was gone. I never saw Samuel again. Life never plays you a fair deal. I was bummed.

DAVID IS CHOSEN
I Samuel 16:1-23

Narrator: Once upon a time, a long time ago, when Saul was king and Samuel was a prophet, there was a man named Jesse and he lived in Bethlehem in the tribe of Judah. One day, God said to Samuel . . .

God: Samuel, it's time to stop grieving over Saul.

Samuel: I feel so terrible. I took all that time to find a king and then he messes up. Woe, Woe, Woe.

God: Pull yourself together. It is I who have rejected him.

Samuel: Okay, I feel better.

God: I wish you to fill your horn with oil and go to Jesse of Bethlehem, for one of his sons shall be king.

Samuel: I have my trusty "Anointing the King Oil Kit" with me and I'm ready to go.

Narrator: So Samuel traveled to Bethlehem and invited Jesse and his sons to a sacrificial feast.

Jesse: Hello, Samuel. Here we are. These are my sons. This is Eliab. Look how tall and handsome he is.

Eliab: Ah, shucks, pop.

Samuel: He doesn't look like Saul or talk like Saul. He must be just right.

God: Appearances don't mean everything. If you could look into his heart, you would know why I have rejected him.

Samuel: Cholesterol problems? And such a young man. A pity.

Jesse: And this is Abinadab. He always helps his poppa.

Samuel: He doesn't look like Eliab and he's not as tall. He must be the new king.

God: I have not chosen this one either.

Samuel: Let me guess. He has dandruff or is it ring around the collar?

Jesse: And this is Shammah. Such a good boy.

God: I have not chosen any of these.

Samuel: I am starting to pick up a pattern here.

Narrator: And one after the other, each of Jesse's sons was rejected. Samuel was about to give up hope when suddenly he asked . . . .

Samuel: Do you have any more sons besides these seven?

Jesse: Well, there's the youngest one. He's out watching the sheep.

Samuel: Bring him to me.

Narrator: Jesse sent for his youngest son, David.

Samuel: He's handsome and bright eyed. He's got ruddy cheeks. Kid, I think I can make you a star.

God: Rise and anoint him, for this is the one.

Narrator: And Samuel anointed David in front of his seven brothers, and the spirit of Adonai was with him from that day forward. But I don't get to say "and they lived happily ever after" because, meanwhile, Saul was possessed with evil spirits.

Saul: I have a major headache. Something is rotten in Israel.

Courtesan: It seems that the evil spirit of God is terrifying you.

Saul: So give me a cure.

Courtesan: We've tried all the major pain relievers. I've heard that music soothes the savage breast.

Saul: Are you calling me a savage?

Courtesan: My, my, the evil spirit is making our king a little touchy.

Saul: Okay, find me someone who is skilled at playing the lyre. Perhaps a little string music will help me relax.

Courtesan: The son of Jesse, the Bethlehemite is skilled in music. He's also a handsome chap.

Saul: Cut the comments and bring the kid to me.

Courtesan: Ooh. That evil spirit is making you a real sourpuss. What ever happened to that party animal that used to sing with the prophets?

Narrator: So David came to Saul, and Saul took a strong liking to him and made him his arms bearer. Whenever the evil spirit of God came upon Saul, David would play his lyre and Saul would relax and feel better.

Courtesan: And we all felt a lot better, too, when Saul wasn't playing King Grouch.

Narrator: But, as I said before, happily ever after it wasn't, because the plot was just beginning to thicken.

DAVID AND GOLIATH

I Samuel 17:1-58

Assistant: I'd like to take a moment to address the studio audience. You are on the set of what we think will be the ultimate epic. As you all know, the Israelites and Philistines are mortal enemies. Today, we are shooting a scene in which champions from each army will fight to the death. Our actors are real – a live Israelite and a live Philistine – because we believe in authenticity. Excuse me for one second. Props, get the artificial turf out of there. We're using natural grass in this scene.

Director: Places, everybody. I want the Philistines massed at Socoh and the Israelites in the Valley of Elah.

Assistant: Everybody is in place.

Director: What about that Philistine champion, what's his face?

Casting: His name is Goliath of Gath. He's a big one. Six cubits and a span tall and loaded down with shekels and shekels of armor. He's the perfect heavy.

Director: Great. Quiet on the set. Focus on the Philistine camp. Do a close-up of Goliath.

Goliath: Why should all of you fight? Choose one of your men and let him come down against me. Um, um . . .

Director: What's the problem?

Goliath: Line, please.

Assistant: If he kills me, we'll be your slaves and if I kill him, you'll be our slaves.

Director: Let's have the Israelites look dismayed and terror stricken. Remember, this brute has been challenging you for forty days. Oh, I love it. Let's take five, everybody.

Eliab: David, what are you doing here?

David: Dad said I could bring some food for you and our other brothers, and I thought it would be fun to be in on the action here.

Shammah: Little bro, this is not the place for you. If they catch you on the set, we could get fired.

David: I brought wine, bread, and cheeses.

Abinadab: I guess you can stay for a little while. Pass the provolone.

Assistant: Quiet on the set.

Goliath: What's the matter with you Israelite wimps?

Director: All right, at this point I want to stage the classic battle of the gladiators. The Israelites will part and out will step He-Man who will engage Goliath in a struggle to the death.

Assistant: Bad news. He-Man is still shooting a film in Thailand and can't be here.

Director: Get someone else.

Assistant: Nobody wants to risk getting hurt fighting Goliath. The stunt men say there isn't enough insurance.

Director: We can't have Goliath ranting and raving for the whole movie. The Israelites need a champion. Go to central casting and find one.

David: How come Goliath is talking like that to the Israelites and nobody is fighting him? He's defying the living God.

Eliab: David, you aren't with the sheep right now. This is the big time. He's just a big Philistine saying his lines. Besides, how would you suggest fighting someone ten times your size?

David: What happens if someone does defeat Goliath?

Assistant: Hey, kid, do you know anyone who might be interested? If someone takes on the role of Israelite champion and wins, he will be rewarded with riches, marry the king's daughter, and not have to pay taxes.

Saul: Step aside. King coming through. Did we get any takers for the starring role yet?

David: I want the part. I know I can be the Israelite champion. Just give me a chance.

Saul: No way. You're just a boy. And besides, you don't look any thing like He-Man. This job requires training. Goliath has been studying his warrior skills for years.

David: I've got experience. When I tended my dad's sheep and a lion or bear attacked, I would always save the flock. I've killed both a lion and a bear. God, who saved me from those beasts, will be with me today. I can do it.

Assistant: I like his style. Costumes and make-up, we need you in the Israelite camp right now.

Saul: You can use my helmet and breastplate. Put the sword over the garment.

David: I can't walk in this stuff. It's too big. I can't relate. Can I use my own materials?

Saul: What do you have?

David: I have a lazer gun.

Assistant: That's too flashy. This is supposed to be ancient.

David: How about my sling shot?

Assistant: It'll be perfect. I must confess, I'm getting kind of excited about this. Its beginning to look like a classic epic.

Director: All right. Clash of the Gladiators, take three. Action.

Goliath: Wait a second. Am I a dog that you come at me with sticks? Is this some kind of joke? Where's He-Man?

David: Stick to your lines, you overgrown beanstalk.

Goliath: I'll mash you up and feed you to the birds.

David: You come against me with sword and spear, but I come against you in the name of the God of Israel whose name you have defamed.

Assistant: Put me down for ten shekels on the sword and spear.

David: On this day, God will deliver you to me and I will kill you and cut off your head. All the earth will know there is a God in Israel.

Director: Tell that kid to stop improvising and stick to the script or we're going to lose our "PG" rating.

Goliath: I thought this was supposed to be an adventure story, not a comedy. I'm going to smash the little twerp.

David: The battle belongs to God and He will deliver you into our hands.

Director: Keep the cameras rolling. David has a stone in his sling shot. He's swinging, swinging, swinging it. Pow! Right into Goliath's forehead. The giant is down. Wait a moment. What is David doing?

Assistant: He's taking Goliath's sword and oooohhhh . . .

Director: I can't believe it. David cut off Goliath's head.

Assistant: How am I going to explain this to Goliath's agent? Maybe we can put him in one of our horror films as an extra.

Director: Keep those cameras rolling. Let's have the Israelites pursuing the Philistines. Philistines — you are in total disarray. Your champion is dead. Run for your lives.

Assistant: I think we have a hit on our hands.

Saul: Young boy, congratulations. Who are you? I must know your name.

David: Don't you recognize me?

Assistant: Our leading man occasionally has laspes. Saul, don't worry; you'll still get top billing.

David: I am David, son of Jesse.

Director: Remember that name, folks. A star is born.

SAUL GROWS JEALOUS
I Samuel 18:1-30

Narrator: David became a commander of the Israelite army and grew popular with the people. And while King Saul began to grow jealous of the young soldier's success, his son Jonathan became David's closest friend.

Jonathan: David, welcome back from battle. How did you do?

David: We had phenomenal success on our mission, Jonathan. Things are going so well. Is your father pleased?

Jonathan: Well, I wouldn't go that far.

David: What do you mean? I am in command of his troops. I am successful on every mission. The troops like me. The court likes me. And I'm best friends with his son.

Jonathan: I just don't think that dad wants to be president of your fan club.

David: You're imagining things.

Jonathan: What about the song that has been number one for the last five weeks? The one that all the women have been singing when we march back home. It goes "Saul has slain his thousands, David his tens of thousands."

David: It's a catchy tune.

Jonathan: Be careful.

David: Relax, I'm going to see your father now. And look . . . I'm wearing the sword and tunic you gave me.

Courtesan: Hear ye, hear ye. The king is now holding court.

Saul: Keep that racket down. Let's have some entertainment.

Courtesan: Very good, sire. Just back from a hit tour and singing their number one single, it's Leah and the Women of Israel.

Leah: May I have an F sharp minor? "Saul has slain his thousands."

Women: "Doo wop doo wop."

Leah: "David his tens of thousands."

Women: "Wop doo wop wop."

Saul: I hate that song. Next thing, you know the runt will want to be king.

Courtesan: Thank you, ladies. That was wonderful. And may I add, what a tasteful selection you chose to sing for King Saul!

Saul: Major headache coming.

Courtesan: Oh, rats. The evil spirit of God is attacking King Saul again. Send for the lyre player.

Assistant: That might not be a good idea. David is the lyre player.

Courtesan: Let's not get all worked up about a little jealousy. David, start playing.

Saul: There's the runt now.

Assistant: Saul just threw his spear at David and barely missed him.

Courtesan: I'm sure he didn't mean it.

Assistant: There goes a second spear and another near miss.

117

Courtesan: Perhaps we ought to end the concert. Thank you, David.

Saul: I've got to get a hold of myself.

Courtesan: Throwing spears at your servant is not a big morale booster.

Saul: I've got to conquer my jealousy. Make David chief of the troops.

Assistant: What a noble gesture.

Saul: That way he has to march at the head of the army and there's a better chance he'll get knocked off.

Gaby: Hello, friends and fellow gossips. This is Gaby Gab in front of King Saul's palace with a report on the wacky world of the wacko king. Today, the adorable David found out that he will not be marrying Princess Merab after all. Even though Saul promised David his oldest daughter, he ended up marrying her off to Adriel the Meholathite. Can you believe it?

Rachel: Rachel Barrett reporting along with Gaby Gab. Gaby, I am shocked. Rumor has it that Adriel has the personality of a goat and smells about the same. Poor Merab. Now, it seems that Saul is going to give David his younger daughter, Michal, who, I hear, has a major crush on our hero.

Gaby: More details later. Right now, this is Gaby Gab and Rachel Barrett with our ears to the palace walls.

Saul: I think I have David where I want him. Go tell him that he can be my son-in-law. What he doesn't know will hurt him.

Servant: King Saul wishes you to marry Michal.

David: But, I'm a poor, humble boy. What could I possibly give King Saul in return?

Servant: I don't think you want to know. Here's our leader now.

Saul: I understand that you have no gift to give me. No problem. Kill one hundred Philistines and that's all I ask.

David: That's it? This is great. I'll be back in no time, Dad!

Saul: Good-bye and good riddance.

Servant: David has returned and he killed two hundred Philistines. He gets to marry Michal.

Michal: My new love.

Jonathan: My new brother.

David: My new family. And a new dad.

Saul: Call me King Dad.

SAUL WANTS A DEAD DAVID
I Samuel 19:1-20:42

Narrator: This is the palace of King Saul, leader of Israel. It is a tormented place where passion and jealousy weave a web of confusion. It's a court where love and hate are one and the same. It is into this nest of human conflict that our two heroes must enter.

Friday: My name is Friday. My partner is Peter Shammos. It was 9:30 a.m. and we entered the residence of the complainant with the tag King Saul.

Saul: Well, it's about time you guys showed up. I want to report a missing person.

Shammos: Description, please.

Saul: Arrogant, status seeking, interested in taking away my kingship.

Friday: Facts, sir. Just the facts.

Saul: Handsome, rugged looks, runs the 40 in 4.6 seconds. He was last seen a few nights ago.

Shammos: Any idea where to start looking?

Saul: Try talking to my son, Jonathan. They're the best of friends. Jonathan doesn't understand that his future as king is threatened so long as David is around.

Friday: Sorry, Mr. King, but politics is not our area. If David is anywhere around here, we'll find him. We'll start with the prince.

Shammos: There's Prince Jonathan in the garden. Son, we have a few questions. Where is your friend David?

Jonathan: David is gone. I don't blame him for taking off. My father hates him. He thinks David wants to be king.

Friday: I'm sure there's more to the story.

Jonathan: I tried telling my old man that David has never done a thing to deserve this hatred. Saul agreed, but his change of heart didn't last for long.

Shabbos: I'm sure that whatever problems there are, your father could talk things out with the missing party.

Jonathan: Well, the last thing Pops did was throw a spear at David. David was playing the lyre during one of the king's spells of madness. And it wasn't the first time that had happened.

Friday: We can deduce that either David is a lousy musician or Saul has trouble verbalizing his musical criticisms. Where is the kid now?

Jonathan: He ran home to his wife.

Shammos: We quickly saddled our donkeys and trotted over to the home of David and Michal. A woman matching the description of Michal answered the door. We began the interrogation using our most subtle approach.

Friday: Okay, lady. Where are you hiding your husband?

Michal: I'm sorry, but David went for a walk.

Shammos: Somehow, we knew she was lying.

Friday: The jig is up. We know the scoop. Spill the beans.

Michal: Please! No more clichés . . . I'll talk. I knew that my father would try to kill him, so I took an idol and put it in David's bed so people would think he was sleeping. Then David slipped out the window and escaped.

Shammos: Your father said that you were forced by David to set up the old "idol in the bed" scam. True or false?

Michal: I lied to Saul and told him David forced me to do it. I love my husband, but have you ever seen my father when he loses his temper? I sure don't want any spears flying my way.

Friday: She was a smart cookie. We were at a dead end. David seemed to have disappeared. Jonathan and Michal were covering his trail. One thought struck us.

Shammos: Samuel. If David is on the up and up, he probably went to see Samuel. Pull the donkeys around and put up the red siren.

Friday: Look, up ahead. There's a band of prophets in ecstasy — trying to communicate with God.

Shammos: Have any of you seen David or Samuel?

Prophet: Officers, Saul is also on their trail. He found out that David went to Ramah to get Samuel and now they're heading toward Naioth. Saul sent out troops to get David, but they joined up with this group of prophets and they're all ranting and raving in ecstasy.

Friday: We better put out a Code 10 alert. Also put out an APB on Saul, David, and Samuel.

Shammos: What's a code 10?

Friday: Growing group of prophets going nutso. Possible disturbance of the peace.

Shabbos: Cancel the APB on Saul. It looks like he's joined the prophets, too.

Friday: This case gets crazier by the minute. Shammos, run for your life. The band of prophets is heading this way.

* * *

David: Psst. Jonathan, over here. In the garden.

Jonathan: David, is that you? Why are you dressed like a bush?

David: Well, besides those bozo agents investigating my disappearance, your father is trying to kill me. I don't even know what I've done wrong.

Jonathan: It can't be. My father wouldn't do anything great or small without letting me know.

David: Oh, darn. Someone has just watered me again. Jonathan, isn't it possible that if your father was going to kill me, he might not tell you since we are best friends?

Jonathan: Gee, do you really think he would do that?

David: Gee, yes! If you don't believe me, let's put my idea to the test. Tomorrow is the new moon and I am supposed to sit with your father at the feast. Tell him I've gone home to be with my family. If he gets angry, you'll know he wishes me harm.

Jonathan: What kind of test is that? If you don't show up to dinner, it would be considered rude. Of course, the king would get angry.

David: Do as I ask. Now, I've got to get out of these bushes and find a new disguise. I'm beginning to mildew.

* * *

Saul: This has been a wonderful festival of the new moon. Where's David?

Jonathan: How about those Giants?

Saul: He's been missing for two days.

Jonathan: The weather certainly has been mild, hasn't it?

Saul: Where is he?

Jonathan: He asked if he could join his family for their annual feast and I told him that it would be okay. I knew you'd be happy to let him go and that it wouldn't really bother you. He has a lot of vacation days coming to him.

Saul: How dare you side with that no-goodnik? As long as he is alive, your kingship is threatened. I want David killed on sight.

Jonathan: I'll agree that his not being here may be rude, but aren't you being rather punitive?

Servant: Oh, please don't let him start throwing spears again.

Jonathan: Pops, you are going to have to do something about your temper. I'm leaving.

Saul: Get back to the table. You haven't eaten anything. Kids — they have no respect.

Friday: This is Friday and Shammos reporting from our undercover assignment of following Prince Jonathan. The suspect is currently walking in the field. He is with a young boy who is carrying arrows. It appears that they are going to practice archery skills.

Shammos: The suspect has sent the boy ahead to retrieve the arrows. The prince seems to be a lousy shot. He's walking toward the top of the hill to meet the boy.

Jonathan: David, where are you?

David: Over here. I'm disguised as a rock.

Jonathan: I sent the boy ahead and nobody knows that we arranged this meeting.

David: Was your father angry that I wasn't there?

Jonathan: What do you mean by angry?

David: Cursing, throwing spears, screaming for my death.

Jonathan: If you put it that way, you could say he was annoyed.

David: I told you that he wanted to kill me.

Jonathan: Whatever happens, we are making a pact that there will always be peace between my house and yours. Now, get going.

David: I could do with a good hug before I leave. This is pretty upsetting.

Friday: The suspect is sobbing like a baby and is hugging a rock.

Shammos: He seems to have developed a strong attachment to that rock.

Friday: Maybe the kid is cracking under the pressure.

Shammos: Like father, like son.

THE PRIESTS OF NOB
I Samuel 21:1-22:23

Narrator: During his flight from the jealous King Saul, David came to the priest Ahimelech at Nob.

Ahimelech: David, is that you?

David: Shh! I'm on a secret mission.

Ahimelech: That explains the Groucho Marx glasses.

David: Me and my boys are in need of certain secret provisions.

Ahimelech: Your boys? But you are alone.

David: It's a clever deception. I have a large number of men hidden in the hills.

Ahimelech: All right, I'll help you. What provisions do you need? Clothes? Arrows?

David: Loaves of bread.

Ahimelech: I only have consecrated bread.

David: Perfect! All I have is consecrated men. Scouts honor. Um. Could I also borrow a sword?

Ahimelech: You don't have a sword? Aren't you a soldier of the king?

David: Sure. I just forgot it. It was the pressure of this secret mission. I have my toothbrush and soap dish, but I forgot to pack my sword.

Ahimelech: We have the sword of Goliath. Would that be sufficient?

David: Goliath's sword? Incredible! I mean, if that's all of you have. Remember, this has to stay between me and you . . . and who's he?

Ahimelech: Doeg the Edomite, King Saul's chief herdsman.

Doeg: Hi, there.

David: I thought we were alone.

Ahimelech: Oops.

Narrator: David then traveled from Nob to Gath, a Philistine city.

Servant: King Achish, there is a rumor that David is in the land.

Achish: The same David who slew Goliath?

Servant: And the one they wrote the song about. "Saul has slain his thousands, David his tens of thousands."

Achish: I hate that song. Especially the "Doo wop, doo wop" part. Go find him.

Friend: David, I don't think it's a good idea to stay with the Philistines.

David: It's one place where Saul won't bother me.

Friend: You're not exactly popular here either. You killed their soldiers and their greatest hero. Your face is on a wanted poster in the city square.

David: Maybe this wasn't such a good idea. I'm going to have to talk to my travel agent about where he sends me.

Servant: David, the king of Gath wants to see you.

Friend: Remember, David, they don't like you.

David: I've got a plan.

Servant: Your highness, I bring you David.

Achish: Are you speaking of that fellow who is scratching at the door and is drooling all over his beard? There are enough crazy men around here. I don't need to add him to our collection. Send him away.

Friend: That was a close call. How did you think of faking madness?

David: I worked for King Saul. I learned from the best.

Narrator: From there, David traveled to the cave of Adullam where his family joined him. Everyone who was in debt and was desperate also joined him. There were four hundred men with him. And David sent his parents to live in Moab to protect them.

Saul: Listen, men of Benjamin. Will this son of Jesse give you fields?

Doeg: Excuse me.

Advisor: Not now. King Saul is trying to work people up against David, even though we can't find him.

Doeg: But, I . . .

Advisor: Shh.

Saul: Will he reward you? Have you made a pact with him like my own son did? I want the runt, and I want him now.

Doeg: Nob.

Saul: What did you call me? Where's my spear?

Advisor: Look out, he has his spear again.

Doeg: No! I saw David in Nob. The priests gave him food and the sword of Goliath.

Saul: Bring me the priests of Nob.

Advisor: Now, remember your temper.

Ahimelech: Gracious king. How can we serve you?

Saul: Did you give David food and a sword?

Ahimelech: Sure. Isn't he your trusted servant?

Saul: I certainly wouldn't call David a trusted servant. He is conspiring to steal my throne and has somehow convinced my son that he's harmless.

Ahimelech: Did I say "servant"? I meant to say "serpent."

Saul: Never kid a kidder.

Ahimelech: We didn't know what David was up to. From now on, we won't help him.

Saul: I know. You're all going to die for your sin.

Ahimelech: Isn't that a bit harsh? How about whipping us, or making us write "I will not help David" a hundred times?

Saul: Guards, kill the holy priests.

Advisor: They refuse to strike down servants of God.

Saul: Doeg, I'll raise your allowance and give you the weekends off.

Doeg: It's a dirty job, but someone has to do it.

Narrator: And Doeg killed eighty-five priests and then he put the town of Nob to sword. Only one son of Ahimelech escaped. Abiathar came to David and told him what had happened. And David swore to protect him.

DAVID AND SAUL PLAY HIDE AND SEEK

I Samuel 23:1-24:23

Narrator: David and his men came to the town of Keilah. Saul found out and summoned all of his troops to go down to Keilah and beseige David and his men.

David: Abiathar, priest of Nob, Saul is coming to attack us. I don't understand King Saul. We just defeated the Philistines who were raiding this town. You would think that Saul would be grateful. But, no, he's still trying to kill me.

Abiathar: I suppose that this feud between the two of you has gone beyond family counseling.

David: Oh, priest with your ephod, answer this question. Would Saul destroy this entire town because of me?

Abiathar: Is the grass green? Is the sky blue? Does a bear . . .

David: All right. You made your point. Considering that we just saved Keilah from the Philistines, is there any chance of these people turning us over to Saul?

Abiathar: Given the choice of total destruction or handing over a man on the "Ten Most Wanted" list, I would say that this town will decide what it will decide.

David: In other words, let's start packing.

Narrator: And now the Bible's most famous game of Hide and Seek begins.

Saul: Yoo hoo, David. I know you're in Ziph and I'm going to find you. One one-thousand . . . five one-thousand, here I come.

David: You can't find me. You can't find me. Na na na na na.

Jonathan: David, my father is getting really close. Find another hiding place.

David: Relax, it's only a game of Hide and Seek.

Jonathan: If he finds you, he'll kill you. He knows that you will be king of Israel and I will be second to you.

Narrator: And now a word to our readers . . . Kids, do not attempt this version of Hide and Seek. Its only for kings and kings to be.

Soldier I: Saul, rumor has it that David is now in Maon.

Saul: Ready or not, here I come.

Advisor I: David, King Saul is going to find us.

David: Nonsense, we're hiding behind a hill.

Advisor I: But Saul is on the other side of the hill.

David: So everytime he circles to one side, we'll circle to the other. That way, he'll never catch us.

Advisor: Is this what we call strategy?

Soldier: King Saul, come quickly. The Philistines have once again invaded the land.

Saul: Why now? Those guys sure know how to ruin a good game of Hide and Seek. King's X. Time Out. We'll have to continue the game later.

Narrator: When Saul returned from pursuing the Philistines, he was told that David was in the wilderness of Ein Gedi.

Saul: Let's stop here for a moment.

General: King Saul, why stop here? We have three thousand men with us and this seems like an unnecessary military precaution.

Soldier I: Do you sense something, sire?

Soldier 2: Is there a breach in the ranks?

General: What strategy have you thought of?

Saul: I have to go to the restroom.

Soldier I: That's a good enough reason to stop.

Saul: I'm going into the cave up ahead.

Soldier 2: We'll wait here.

Advisor I: David, this is a great hiding place. Saul will never look inside this cave.

David: I hope not. Uh, oh. Someone is coming into the cave.

Advisor 2: It's Saul. How did he know where to look? He sure is good at Hide and Seek.

Advisor: Why is he stopping? Has he a master plan?

David: Actually, it looks like he has taken our cave to be a shady resting place. He doesn't suspect that we are here.

Advisor 2: This is the day which Adoni spoke of when God promised to deliver your enemy into your hand.

David: I have an idea. Give me that knife. I'll return shortly.

Advisor I: This is it! David finally is going to fight back.

David: I did it.

Advisor 2: What did you do?

David: I cut off the corner of Saul's cloak.

Advisor 1: That sure will teach him a lesson.

Advisor 2: You certainly showed him a thing or two. Can we finish him off or do you think that the damage done to his wardrobe will be punishment enough?

David: What have I done? I feel terrible. Getting down to his level is wrong. He is God's anointed.

Narrator: Saul left the cave and started on his way. Then David also went out of the cave and called after Saul.

David: My lord King.

Saul: Cut the bowing routine. What do you want?

David: Why do you listen to people who say that I am out to hurt you?

Saul: It's only polite to listen to others at the dinner table.

David: I could have killed you today. In fact, I was urged to, but I didn't. Take a look at your cloak.

Saul: Hey, the corner is torn. I've got to talk to my tailor about not using cheap materials. But why are we discussing my wardrobe?

David: I have that corner in my hand, for I cut it off while you slept. If I had wanted to kill you, I could have.

Saul: You sneaked up and cut my garment in the cave?

David: As the ancient proverb says, "Wicked deeds come from wicked men." I will never harm you.

Saul: You're right, David. It's just that sometimes I get carried away.

Advisor 1: That's an understatement.

Saul: You've done nothing, yet I have treated you badly. A man who meets his enemy would not let him go on his way.

Advisor 2: By George, I think he's got it.

Saul: I just want you to swear that one day when you are king, you will not harm the descendants of my house.

David: Consider it done. Farewell, King Saul.

Advisor I: Wonderful. I guess we can all pack for home now that peace has been made.

David: Considering Saul's temper and his memory, do you think that would be a wise move?

Advisor 2: All right, men. Let's go find another hideout. This time, look for a place that doesn't have "Rest Spot" printed over the entrance.

NABAL AND ABIGAIL
I Samuel 25:1-44

Narrator: There was a man in Maon whose possessions were in Carmel. The man was very wealthy — he owned three thousand sheep and a thousand goats. His name was Nabal and his wife was Abigail. Abigail was beautiful and intelligent. Nabal, on the other hand, was uh, um . . .

Nabal: Keep shearing those sheep.

Servant 1: We need a break.

Nabal: You get fifteen minutes off every other Tuesday. Let's not get lazy. Back to work.

Servant 2: Nabal, our minds are elsewhere. Samuel the prophet has died and our thoughts drift toward Ramah where they have buried him.

Nabal: Why should just your thoughts drift toward Ramah? You can go there yourself.

Servant 2: I can?

Nabal: Sure, you're fired.

Servant 2: But I need this job.

Nabal: All right, you're rehired, but at half your original salary.

Servant 1: Look, messengers are approaching.

Messenger: David has sent the ten of us to greet you in his name.

Nabal: I'm impressed. Now, if you'll excuse me, there is sheep shearing to be done.

Messenger: That's why we are here. As you know, we protected your shepherds in the wilderness. No harm came to them. Ask them and they will tell you.

Nabal: Is there a point to this conversation? I want to get back to harassing my servants.

Messenger: Receive us warmly for we have come with good intention. Give to us and to David any provisions you can.

Nabal: This is a joke, right? We're all laughing? Where's the hidden camera?

Messenger: We come as messengers of David.

Nabal: David? Who is this guy? You all look like a bunch of runaway slaves. You want me to take the food I have made for my own shearers and give it to men who come from I don't know where?

Messenger: Should we take that as a "no"?

Nabal: Give the kid a lollipop. He figured it out. Now, go away.

Messenger: Are we catching him on a bad day?

Servant 2: Actually, this is one of the boss man's better ones.

Narrator: The young men retraced their steps to David and told him what had happened.

David: Nabal certainly seems to have an attitude problem.

Messenger: What shall we do?

David: We are going to teach Nabal a little lesson in manners. Gather four hundred men in battle gear. By daybreak, there will not be a single member of Nabal's household alive.

Messenger: You call that a "little" lesson in manners? I'm glad I'm on your side.

Narrator: Meanwhile, back at Nabal's house, the beautiful and intelligent Abigail was lounging around when a servant arrived.

Servant 3: We ran into some old friends today.

Abigail: I didn't know Nabal had any old friends . . . or any new friends, for that matter.

Servant 3: They were men from David's band of warriors. Do you know of David?

Abigail: That handsome, ruddy looking hunk of a hero who kills Philistines and whipped Goliath?

Servant 3: Yes.

Abigail: I can't say that I do.

Servant 3: David protected us in the wilderness. He never took anything from us while we tended the flocks. Now, when David asks for provisions, Nabal turns him down. I think there will be trouble. I fear that harm threatens our master.

Abigail: Nabal's a nasty old man. There's not a moment to lose.

Chef: Madam Abigail. What a lovely suprise! Do you wish to go over tomorrow's menu?

Abigail: No, I just dropped by to pick up a few things for a ride in the country.

Chef: What do you need?

Abigail: Two hundred loaves of bread, two jars of wine, five dressed sheep, five seahs of corn, one hundred raisin cakes, and two hundred fig cakes.

Chef: Are you serious?

Abigail: You have no idea how exercise increases a gal's appetite.

Narrator: Abigail had the supplies loaded on donkeys and she ordered her servants to lead them down the trail. But she did not tell Nabal. After all, she was intelligent.

David: We're going to massacre that old grouch. We protected his property for nothing.

Soldier: Look ahead, David. There is a train of donkeys coming this way.

David: Forget the donkeys. Look at the lady. She is beautiful.

Narrator: And she is intelligent, too.

Abigail: Master, please let your handmaid speak.

David: Go ahead. I like a lady with moxy.

Abigail: Pay no attention to that rotten wretched man Nabal.

David: What wrong has he done you?

Abigail: He married me. Did you know that Nabal means "boor." His parents must have known what he'd be like.

Soldier: Yet, he changed his mind and sent the food.

Abigail: I bring the food. I didn't see your messengers when they arrived. Please do not spill innocent blood. God has granted you an enduring house because you fight for good.

David: Has anyone ever told you that you are not just beautiful but intelligent?

Abigail: Thank you. What would you really have done if I hadn't brought you the food?

David: I would have destroyed every member of your household.

Abigail: In that case, a double thank-you.

Narrator: Abigail went home to Nabal. Nabal was having a feast fit for a king and was in a merry mood, so she did not tell him anything at all until . . . daybreak.

Nabal: Ouch, my head.

Abigail: Good morning, darling.

Nabal: Are you talking to me?

Abigail: You are my husband and I am concerned about you.

Nabal: If you are so concerned, how about finding me some raisin cakes. I'd like breakfast, but we seem to be out of everything.

Abigail: Sit down, Nabal. I have the cutest story to tell you. I went on a picnic yesterday and bumped into David, son of Jesse. He and his men were hungry and I happened to have enough food, so they joined me for the picnic.

Nabal: How dare you defy me!

Abigail: He was on his way to kill you and our entire household.

Nabal: Um, um, um, aaah.

Abigail: Nabal, you're changing color. Are you okay?

Messenger: David, word comes from Carmel that Nabal has died. Abigail told him that she gave you all that food and he had a stroke.

David: I'd say I'm sorry to hear it, but I'd hate to be called a liar. There's only one thing to do. I need my scribe.

Messenger: Will I be sent to deliver a condolence note?

David: Why? Did something sad happen?

Narrator: And David sent his messengers to Abigail.

Messenger: Abigail, I bring you news from David.

Abigail: Please tell me. But let me first sit down. I am a lady in mourning.

Messenger: Our master would like to marry you.

Abigail: Saddle up the horses, pack my bags, and let's make time.

Messenger: So you are saying "yes"?

Abigail: I'm not just another pretty face. I'm also intelligent. I know a good deal when I see one.

Narrator: Besides Abigail, David had also taken Ahinoam of Jezreel, so both of them became his wives. Meanwhile, Saul gave his daughter, Michal, David's wife, to Palti son of Laish of Gallim.

DAVID BEFRIENDS THE PHILISTINES
I Samuel 26:1-28:2

David: This is the life. Married with two wives and living with my merry men in the wilderness of Ziph, we rob from the rich and give to the poor. And all the time, we hide from King Saul.

Soldier: Before you get too carried away, David Hood, you should know that King Saul and Abner, the Sheriff of Canaan, are fast approaching with three thousand of their finest soldiers.

David: Call my trusted counselors and friends, Ahimelech and Abishai.

Ahimelech: We hear that there is trouble in the wilderness.

David: Yes, but I have a scheme. Who will go down into Saul's camp with me?

Abishai: I'll go.

Ahimelech: I'll go.

David: Thank you, lads. Little Abishai spoke first so he shall go. Big Ahimelech, take care of Lady Abigail and Lady Ahinoam. Fare thee well.

Abishai: Look, the entire camp is asleep. There is the evil King Saul with his spear in the ground at his head. Let us give him a splitting headache.

David: Nay, my friend. He will die in battle in his own time. I am forbidden to touch one of God's anointed. However, let us have some merry fun. Take his spear and water jug.

Narrator: And David crossed over to the other side and stood off afar on top of a hill.

David: Hello, you cursed knaves. And a special hello to you, Sheriff Abner.

Abner: David Hood. You are a thief and scoundrel. Who are you to shout at King Saul?

David: You should watch your beloved leader a little more carefully. You deserve to die for not being on guard. Where are the king's water jug and spear?

Abner: Forsooth, you took them. David Hood, you are no good.

Saul: Is that David?

David: It is David, and I resent Abner's accusations. I am a good hood. Why do you pursue me again? I am a loyal servant of the king.

Saul: You are right, David. Come back, for I will not harm you since you spared my life once again.

David: Here is your spear. Send someone to get it. Now I must be off. I hope that God will reward me someday, for I valued your life. And then I shall be rescued from all this trouble.

Saul: You will be blessed and you shall prevail. Fare thee well.

David: And now, Little Abishai, it's back to our band of merry men.

Abishai: But our happy little wilderness is not safe anymore.

David: Verily, you're right. Let us gather up the men and seek haven in the land of the Philistines. Saul will not pursue us there.

Narrator: So David Hood and his merry men and ladies crossed over to King Achish of Gath and was granted the town of Ziklag in which to live.

David: Big Ahimelech, how did the raid go today?

Ahimelech: Our men destroyed two Amalekite towns.

Abishai: With our destruction of the Amalekite, Geshurite, and Gizrite towns, we're getting rich.

David: And the King of Gath thinks that we are stealing from Israelites. But, nay, we steal from the heathen and give to Israel.

Ahimelech: Let's celebrate with ale and mutton and archery contests. And we can have Avi of Dale sing songs of our noble deeds.

Abishai: Who knows? Someone might write a book someday about us and call it "David Hood and His Merry Men."

All: Naaaaahhhh.

Messenger: David, word comes from the king of Gath. He wants you to join him in his battle against the Israelites.

David: He thinks that we have been attacking our own people and have, therefore, earned their hatred.

Messenger: What should I tell Achish?

David: Tell him that he knows what his servant will do. Let him appoint me his bodyguard. Now, let the minstrel play a tune.

Minstrel: "Saul has slain his thousands, David his tens of thousands."

David: I love that song. "Doo wop, doo wop."

SAUL AND THE WITCH
I Samuel 28:3-25

Soldier 1: Here it is, the En-dor Inn.

Soldier 2: This is kind of spooky.

Soldier 1: It's supposed to be spooky. We're looking for a lady who talks to ghosts.

Soldier 2: I thought Saul had forbidden people to talk to ghosts and spirits. It is supposed to be against the law.

Soldier 1: What is Saul going to do? Arrest himself and then put himself on trial in front of himself . . .

Soldier 2: Okay, okay. Shhh. Here comes Saul. He doesn't look so good.

Saul: Is this the place?

Soldier 1: This is the home of the lady that consults ghosts.

Witch: Who is at the door?

Saul: I need you to divine a ghost for me.

Witch: Are you crazy? Keep your voice down. It's against the law. That idiot King Saul banned it.

Saul: As God lives, you won't get in trouble for this.

Witch: Okay, enough with the begging. Who shall I bring up for you?

Saul: Samuel.

Witch: For goodness sake, the man just died. Give him a chance to unpack.

Saul: I must speak to Samuel.

Witch: Wait a minute. You look familiar. Didn't you star in the *Book of Judges* ?

Saul: I don't think so.

Witch: Wait . . . you're . . . King Saul.

Soldier 1: Oh, no! We've been found out.

Soldier 2: Relax. I doubt that she's going to be making a citizen's arrest.

Saul: Don't be afraid. Tell me what you see.

Witch: It's coming to me now . . . . I see an old man . . . in a robe.

Saul: It's Samuel.

Samuel: What's the problem? I haven't been gone for a week and already I'm getting business calls. I'm retired.

Saul: Samuel, I'm in trouble. The Philistines are getting ready to attack and God has turned away from me. He no longer answers me, either by prophets or by dreams.

Witch: Oy, are you in trouble!

Saul: Why has God turned away from me?

Samuel: Where should we begin? You ignored God's instructions. That was bad. Then, you didn't kill all of the Amalekites as you were commanded. That was worse.

Saul: What can I do to repent?

Samuel: Nothing. Well, I'll see you tommorrow.

Saul: I am not coming to this place again.

Samuel: Actually, you are. You and your sons will be killed by the Philistines and all of Israel will suffer defeat. By the way, I left my toothbrush on my night table. Could you bring it with you?

Witch: He's gone. Aren't you glad you had a chance to talk to Samuel? You must feel much better. That will be ten shekels.

Soldier 2: I think he fainted.

Witch: Of course. It looks like he hasn't had a good meal all day. Listen, your majesty. You can't keep going on an empty stomach.

Saul: What's the point? This has been a terrible day.

Soldier 1: Look at the cheery side, sire. There's always tomorrow.

Witch: I can tell that your job as bodyguard doesn't require much intelligence.

Soldier 2: We'll have some of your bread and fresh meat, but then we must leave in the night.

Samuel: And don't forget my toothbrush.

SAUL'S LAST STAND

I Samuel 29:1-31:13

Lord I: Have all the Philistine lords arrived with their troops?

Lord 2: They are still coming. We can sense victory in the air. King Saul will wish the sun had never come up today.

Lord 3: Here comes King Achish and his men.

Lord 1: I also recognize David, the servant of Saul, and his Israelite warriors.

Lord 2: David? What's he doing here?

Achish: Relax, he's on our side.

Lord 1: This is David who slew Goliath. The same fellow who killed two hundred of our soldiers as a wedding present. The same guy of whom they sing "Saul has slain his thousands, David his tens of thousands."

Lord 3: "Doo wop, doo wop." It sort of gets to you.

Achish: Hey, people change.

Lord 2: Achish, wake up and smell the pomegranates. If David's in this fight, we're taking our marbles and going home.

Achish: David, I need to speak with you. I have bad news.

David: Would it have something to do with all those Philistine lords shaking their swords at me?

Achish: David, don't take this personally. I know you are loyal to me. However, some of the other guys seem to think

147

you might betray them. It has to do with the Goliath thing.

David: You make a few mistakes and, wham — you're labeled for life. Achish, I understand. I guess I won't get to fight against my own people. Shucks and dagnabbit.

Achish: I know you would have fought. Here are some shekels. Go take your warriors out for breakfast. The Philistines want you out of here by dawn.

David: Farewell, Achish. Thanks for the omelet money. Bye.

Warrior I: David, were we really going to fight on the side of the Philistines? I know that Saul has been wacko, but it would still have seemed unpatriotic.

David: Relax. You can still proudly raise the old blue and white in the air. I knew the Philistines wouldn't let us join them. It was a trick.

Warrior 2: Did the Philistines react the way you thought they would?

David: Totally. I wish the Brooklyn Bridge was already built so I could sell it to Achish. Let's head back to Ziklag.

Narrator: And David and his warriors rose in the morning to leave, to return to the land of the Philistines, while the Philistines marched up to Jezreel.

Warrior 2: Home sweet home.

Warrior 3: It would be if we could find it.

David: Did we lose our direction? Ziklag should be where we left it.

Warrior I: Look over there. It's been burned to the ground. They've taken our women and children. And there's a note. It reads: On the third day, while you were away, we thought we'd come over for a bite. You left your families alone, didn't bother to phone, so we took them. Love, the Amalekites.

David: Those doity rats. They took my sweet Ahinoam and Abigail.

Warrior 2: Your men may take this out on you if something isn't done.

David: Why do you say that?

Warrior 3: They're picking up stones and walking this way.

David: Gentlemen, and I use the term loosely.

Warrior 2: Why'd you say that?

David: It's always good to warm up the crowd with a joke.

Warrior 1: They're not laughing.

David: I have consulted our priest, Abiathar, and God has promised to deliver the Amalekites to us.

All: Hooray!

David: It's also important to have a strong ending to your speech.

Narrator: David and his men gave chase until they reached Wadi Besor. There he left two hundred men who were too tired to go on and continued with four hundred warriors.

Warrior 1: There is the Amalekite camp.

Warrior 2: It was lucky we came across that Egyptian slave that they had left behind. How did you get him to talk?

David: I made him an offer he couldn't refuse.

Warrior 3: What was that?

David: If he told us where they were, he got to live.

Warrior 1: Check out all the spoils they have. Those

Amalekites have been very busy little thieves. They seem to be having quite a party down there.

David: Not for long. Attack!

Narrator: And David rescued everything that the Amalekites had taken. Nobody had been injured. He forced the soldiers to share the spoils with those who had waited at Wadi Besor. And this became a fixed rule for Israel that all share in the spoils. Meanwhile, in the northern part of Israel . . .

Saul: Circle the wagons. Keep firing your arrows in rounds.

Soldier: It's no good, sire. We are totally surrounded by the Philistines.

Saul: If we hold out, maybe my sons Jonathan, Abinadab, or Malchishua will be able to break through and join ranks.

Soldier: That would be very difficult for them to do at this time, sire.

Saul: They're good soldiers.

Soldier: I am sorry to break this to you, but they *were* good soldiers. They are now. . . my sympathies, sire.

Saul: Perhaps, we can get one of our men through the lines to go for help.

Soldier: I hate to be a pessimist, but we're the only ones left. You are badly hurt. I can't leave you.

Saul: Draw your sword and end it for me. I don't want the Philistines to capture me.

Soldier: I can't do it.

Saul: That figures. I have to do everything myself.

Soldier: Hey, I'm not staying here alone. If you're falling on your sword, so am I. There go my retirement plans.

Narrator: On that day, Saul, his three sons, his arms bearer, and all his men died together. The Israelites saw this and fled, and the Philistines occupied their towns. The people of Jabesh-Gilead came out and buried the bodies of Saul and his son which the Philistines had put on display. And then they fasted for seven days.

DAVID LAMENTS SAUL'S DEATH
II Samuel 1:1-27

Attendant: David, it's almost time for your turn in the talent show.

David: I just have to tune the lyre. When do I go on?

Attendant: First are the sheep jugglers and then comes the guy who does impersonations of false gods. It's your turn after him.

Assistant: I'm very sorry, sir, but David can not be disturbed right now.

Soldier: But I have very important news for him.

Assistant: Every fan does. Do you see that six pointed star on the door? That means that the person behind the door is important and may not be bothered by autograph seekers.

Soldier: I'm not a member of David's fan club.

Assistant: And why not? David is the hottest show in Israel right now. Not even King Saul's spear throwing act is more popular.

Soldier: Well, definitely not anymore. I come from the battlefield with news of the king.

David: I heard that. Come in and tell me what happened.

Attendant: Five minutes to curtain. They just finished cleaning up the stage after the sheep jugglers.

Soldier: Say, what a nice room. Do you need a personal assistant?

David: This is no time to worry about your career. Are Saul and Jonathan dead?

Soldier: I was with him at Mount Gilboa. We were surrounded by the enemy. Saul was wounded and bloodied and covered with dirt. Let's face it, he'd had better days. He looked over to me and asked my name.

David: I'm beginning to wonder that myself.

Soldier: I tell him that I'm an Amalekite and he begs me to finish him off, which I did. And now I bring you his crown and armlet. Let me be the first to call you king.

David: Saul is dead. You shall be punished.

Soldier: Me? I just bumped off the guy who has been trying to kill you.

David: I want this man struck down.

Soldier: This is not what I call gratitude.

David: You thought you were bringing me good news, but you are wrong. How did you dare kill God's anointed?

Soldier: Did I say that? I was mistaken. He fell on his own sword. Honest. I have these memory lapses. Oops, here comes another one . . . who are you? . . . where am I?

David: Take him away.

Soldier: Does this mean I don't get the job as your personal assistant?

Assistant: David, the crowd is waiting for you. You're on next.

Comedian: My final impersonation is of the false god, Malech. Umm, I want some dinner. How about some kiddie-bits? Get it? You know . . . child sacrifice?

Attendant: Thank you for that fine impersonation. We look forward to seeing this young talent again . . . maybe in Eygpt.

153

And now, the final act in our Ziklag Talent Show is none other than David, son of Jesse.

David: Ladies and gentlemen. Tonight, I found out that our king and his son, Jonathan, my best friend, were killed in battle. I would like to dedicate this dirge to them. Can you introduce me again?

Attendant: And now, our final act is none other than Mr. David, son of Jesse, loyal subject to King Saul and best friend of Prince Jonathan.

David: I dedicate this song to them. It's called "How the Mighty Have Fallen." I'd like to play it now.

Assistant: This is so sad. The entire crowd is weeping and mourning.

David: O hills of Gilboa, let there be no dew or rain on you. There the shield of warriors lay rejected, the shield of Saul, polished with oil no more.

Attendant: Oh, I want a copy of this song. It's so sad, but, oh, so beautiful.

Assistant: It's in the Book of Jashar. They're selling copies in the lobby.

Attendant: Pass the tissue paper.

WHO IS THE KING?
II Samuel 2:1-3:39

Narrator: After speaking with God, David decided to go up to the town of Hebron in the territory of his tribe of Judah. The men of Judah came and there they anointed David as king of Judah. A historian assesses the situation.

Historian: You are now asking yourself a question. Hey, self, why wasn't David crowned king of all of Israel? But, as anyone who has ever worked a Rubic's Cube knows, nothing is ever as easy as it looks. Saul had a son named Ishbosheth who was crowned king. He was supported by General Abner. King David was crowned king and was supported by General Joab. What we have here is a civil war. Are you tired of this history lesson? Me, too. Let's turn on the television.

M.C.: Welcome to the new biblical version of "To Tell the Truth." Let's introduce our guest panelists who will try to determine who is pulling our leg and who is the real personality. Okay, Yochanan, who do we have?

Yochanan: First, we have that great officer from Saul's army, General Abner of Ner.

M.C.: Abner, thanks for taking time out from your busy schedule. What are you doing now that King Saul is gone?

Abner: I am currently serving Saul's son and successor, Ishbosheth.

Historian: Personally, I like Abner. He is a very honest and loyal man even if he has lousy luck with the kings he serves.

Yochanan: Next, we have the rock star Leah who made it big with her number one song "Saul has killed his thousands, David his tens of thousands."

Abner: I hate that song.

M.C.: Leah, how's the music scene?

Leah: Well, we've been touring the Fertile Crescent. Things around here have been too messy with this civil war going on.

Historian: We don't read about Leah the rock star in the Bible. I think it was a good idea not to include her. She only had one hit song.

Yochanan: And finally, we have Joab — military advisor to David.

Historian: Joab is loyal, but his temper is legendary and he can be very sneaky. I've heard that even his mother frisks him before he leaves her house.

M.C.: Joab, you appear to be quite busy these days.

Joab: As you know, David has been crowned king of Judah. Watching out for his interests is taking up a lot of my time.

Abner: David's an imposter. Ishbosheth is the king. He rules over all of Israel except one tribe.

Joab: Says who?

Leah: Oh gross. Two grown men are about to get into a fight over a silly little thing like who is the rightful king of Israel. It's such a typical macho attitude.

M.C.: Panelists, this is a game show, not a boxing exhibition. Please control yourselves.

Joab: All right, let's get on with this stupid game.

M.C.: We are about to hear from two guests. One of them is an imposter. Let's listen to their introductions.

David: My name is David and I am king of Israel.

Ishbosheth: My name is Ishbosheth and I am king of Israel.

Leah: What kind of name is Ishbosheth? It doesn't rhyme with any lyrics at all.

Joab: I vote for David.

M.C.: Wait a minute, we haven't heard their stories yet.

Leah: I may vote for Ishbah, Ishta, Ishboth . . . for the guy with the long name.

M.C.: Everybody calm down. I want to remind our panelists that this is not the way we play the game. First, you hear two conflicting stories and then, and only then, you decide who is telling the truth. If you aren't willing to play the game properly, there will be no prizes. Leah, Abner, and Joab are you willing to play the game or not?

Abner: But I already know who is telling the truth.

Joab: It's David!

Abner: Liar! It's Ishbosheth! Draw your sword.

M.C.: Cut to a commercial.

Yochanan: Not on your life. The ratings will go through the roof on this one.

Historian: Civil war is a dirty business.

Narrator: Ishbosheth was forty years old when he became king of Israel. But the House of Judah supported David. The war between the House of Saul and the House of David was long and drawn out, but David kept getting stronger.

* * *

Referee: Now, boys. I'm going to have to caution both of you. This civil war is supposed to be a clean fight. Each of you has been caught cheating.

Abner: I haven't cheated.

Joab: What do you call it when you killed my brother Asahel?

Abner: He was a klutz. After the last battle he kept chasing us. So, I stuck my sword out and he ran right into it.

Referee: Back to your corners.

Rizpah: Abner, here is some cold water. You look great out there.

Abner: Thanks a lot. Give me a kiss for good luck.

Ishbosheth: What is Rizpah doing here? She was my father, King Saul's girlfriend. I am very disappointed in you Abner. You should not have brought her.

Abner: I can't believe this. I have supported you and the House of Saul. I have been your number one boxer. We are fighting for the championship crown. And you are criticizing me for my choice of dates!

Referee: I hate to interrupt this lovely conversation, but the bell has rung and only one fighter is in the ring. Would you like to join us?

Abner: Ishbosheth, I am throwing in the towel. I'm fed up with you as a manager. I'm switching sides. King David, can you use another hand?

Narrator: And David said that he would make a pact with Abner if the general would appear with Michal, daughter of Saul. And Michal, for whom David paid the bride price of one hundred slain Philistines, was brought to him.

David: Joab, I know you'd like to continue fighting Abner because of that little incident.

Joab: Little incident? He killed my brother.

David: Let's not lose our temper. He's brought me back my wife and has told me that Israel and even Saul's tribe of

Benjamin now support me. As a matter of fact, I'm calling off the fight.

Joab: Ring the bell.

Referee: Sorry, but it looks like this fight is being cancelled.

Joab: That's not fair. Ring the bell.

David: Hang up the gloves, Joab. Abner is switching sides and supporting us. There's nobody left to fight.

Narrator: Joab was angered when he heard that Abner had come to King David and had walked away unharmed. Joab followed Abner to Hebron and drew him aside as if to talk privately with him. There he stabbed him in the belly.

Referee: Joab, what did you do? A knife in the belly is a flagrant violation of the rules. This fight was officially over. Go back to your corners. Well, Abner, you can stay where you are.

David: You killed Abner when he was coming over to our side.

Referee: David, I will have to report this to the commission. I hope you will reprimand your fighter.

David: I will curse him and his family. And I will force him to mourn for Abner. Now, Joab, go to bed without dinner.

Narrator: The troops buried Abner in Hebron and David mourned the loss of this great man of Israel by fasting on that day. All Israel knew that it was not by David's will that Abner was killed.

THE END OF SAUL'S HOUSE
II Samuel 4:1-12

Narrator: When Ishbosheth, son of King Saul, heard that Abner, his general, had died in Hebron, he lost heart. Now, two of his company commanders, Baanah and Rechab, decided to make the best of a bad situation.

Baanah: Are you sure we are doing the right thing?

Rechab: What's the point of being on the losing side? Nobody is supporting Ishbosheth anymore.

Baanah: That's for sure. They can't even pronounce his name.

Servant: Where are you two going?

Baanah: I'm Baanah and this is Rechab. Don't you recognize us? We're company commanders.

Servant: Is that why you have all those swords and knives?

Rechab: Right. We're just going inside the palace to get some wheat.

Servant: Okay. Loyal subjects are always welcome to enter. But all of us must be on guard. Rumors are circulating that there are those who might want to assassinate Ishbosheth.

Baanah: Pshaw! That's absurd. Who would want to kill our magnificent and noble leader?

Servant: Are we talking about the same person? He's afraid of his own shadow now that his General Abner is gone.

Rechab: We'll be right back.

Servant: You're going the wrong way. The kitchen is in the back. You're heading toward the king's bedchamber.

Baanah: We wanted to take the long way past the king's room. We need the exercise. After all, we have a war to lose.

Servant: For a moment, I thought you were . . . oh, all right, go ahead. I guess I'm seeing assassins under every rock.

Rechab: Knock, knock. Ishbosheth, can we come in?

Ishbosheth: I'm trying to sleep.

Baanah: Sire, we have figured out a way to end the war.

Ishbosheth: The war is lost. You can do what you want.

Rechab: We appreciate your blessing.

Narrator: Rechab and Baanah stabbed Ishbosheth to death while he slept in his bedchamber. They then beheaded him.

Mephiboshet: Where are those thugs going?

Servant: Mephibosheth, you surprise me. They're your uncle's soldiers and they're picking up some wheat.

Mephiboshet: I may be only five, but I don't think they mean well.

Servant: Don't be silly. Your father Jonathan would not have liked to hear you accuse people of bad things.

Mephiboshet: Why are those soldiers leaving so quickly? And that sack they carry doesn't look like it has wheat in it. It's dripping red stuff on the floor.

Narrator: Rechab and Baanah brought the head of Ishbosheth to David in Hebron.

Rechab: Here's an early birthday present. Now you are avenged against the House of Saul and his offspring.

David: This reminds me of a story.

Baanah: David is taking us into his confidence. He only tells stories to those he trusts.

David: A man thought he was bringing me good news when he told me that Saul was dead.

Rechab: That man sounds like a great guy. Where is he? We share something in common. We'd like to meet him.

David: You will. I seized him and killed him.

Baanah: We don't have to meet him that soon.

David: The earth shall be rid of you and your evil.

Rechab: It was an accident.

David: You stabbed a blameless man in the belly while he slept and then cut off his head.

Baanah: Okay, it was a clumsy accident.

David: Nice try.

Narrator: And David gave orders to execute Rechab and Baanah and he buried Ishbosheth in the grave of Abner in Hebron.

DAVID IS ANOINTED KING
II Samuel 5:1-25

Narrator: All the tribes of Israel came to David in Hebron and said: We are your own flesh and blood. You shall be ruler of Israel.

Manager: David, I'm here to brief you on a few items.

David: Who are all these people with you?

Manager: Image makers! You're going to be king of all Israel, not just of the tribe of Judah. This is the major leagues and you aren't a little shepherd boy anymore.

David: Let's make this meeting fast. I've got be at to the official anointing by the elders of Israel.

Wardrobe: You're not going anywhere in that tunic. That color is all wrong. Redheads don't wear mauve. Besides, it makes you look too young.

David: I am young.

Wardrobe: We want to cover that up. You have to look like a very stately thirty year old.

Manager: Follow the instructions and you'll be king for forty years.

David: We'll finish this meeting later. Let's gather here after the anointing ceremony.

Advisor 1: You're not thinking of keeping Hebron as your capital city, are you?

David: I like Hebron.

Advisor 1: David, David, David. You need a town that is on neutral ground. Judah might be your favorite tribe, but you have to create a more nationalistic image.

David: I hate moving. You have to send out all those change of address cards, collect boxes, and rent a donkey cart U-Haul. Besides, where would we place the capital?

Advisor 1: Our people have come up with the ideal site. The new capital should be Jerusalem.

David: There's a problem with that.

Advisor 1: What's that?

David: The Jebusites live there and they might not like being kicked out of the town they built. They've sworn that we will never enter their city. Even their blind and lame will fight us.

Manager: David, you're a warrior. You will capture the city. Trust me. The tribes will love it. Their king scores a military victory over the obnoxious Jebusites.

Advisor 2: We have been working on a new name for the new capital, something really classy.

David: Why don't we just call it Jerusalem? People are used to it.

Advisor 2: We are talking image here!

David: I've got it. Let's call it the City of David.

Advisor 2: That's stupid. It's too simple. It'll never fly.

David: I like it.

Advisor 2: On the other hand, the concept is simple, yet bold. What a great name. I love it. Doesn't everybody just love it?

Manager: And here is a picture of how your new home in the City of David is going to look. Hiram of Tyre is personally seeing to its construction.

David: Wow! This is too good to be true. There has to be a catch. What are the interest rates? How long is escrow? What kind of commission is the real estate agent taking?

Advisor 1: David, you are the king. All puns aside, it's on the house.

Manager: We've taken care of your image as David the builder, David the warrior, and David the anointed king. However, there's one area we don't want to overlook.

Advisor 3: You are about to become David the lover. We want your face on all the gossip magazines, like *Anashim* or *Anachnu*.

David: Was King Saul in these magazines?

Manager: No, and that was his problem. He was usually on the cover of *Psychology Today*. We want you to be adored. And remember, because of all these wars, women make up the majority of the population.

Advisor 4: Could everyone please come in here?

David: Who are all these people?

Advisor 4: These are your new wives and handmaidens.

David: All of them?

Advisor 4: It's tough being a king. Here is a list of suitable names for all the kids you're going to have.

David: When am I going to have time to be king?

Manager: How about starting now? The Philistines are about to attack us. They're not too thrilled about you being king of Israel. After all, you're the guy that gave their hero Goliath a major headache and killed a hundred Philistines as a bridal gift.

David: To arms. God will deliver the Philistines into our hands.

Wardrobe: You're not going to war in *that* outfit.

David: Fighting the Philistines is the one thing I can handle without this entourage. Out of my way or you shall serve as practice targets. Nobody told me that when I became king I'd have to worry about wardrobe.

Manager: At least, let us get a sketch of you looking kingly as you prepare for battle. Um . . . are you pointing that arrow at me, your majesty? Okay, everybody, I think this session is over.

Narrator: David marched against the Philistines and defeated them. Once again, the Philistines gathered in the Valley of Rephaim and David routed them from Geba all the way to Gezer.

THE ARK ENTERS THE CITY
II Samuel 6:1-23

David: The time has come to bring the Ark of God to my city.

Advisor: The Ark has great power. Have you taken precautions?

David: I've brought thirty thousand men with me.

Advisor: That should do it.

Uzza: Hello, I'm Uzza and this is my brother Ahio. We're from the Holy Ark Moving and Storage Company.

David: You're going to be bringing the Ark of God to the City of David.

Ahio: Uh, according to the order, we're taking it to Jerusalem.

Advisor: Same difference.

David: Are you familiar with the Ark?

Ahio: Kind of. It's been stored at our father Abinadab's house for a long time.

Uzza: We've got a new cart parked outside.

David: Remember not to touch the Ark while it's moving.

Uzza: Hey, we know our business. We're professionals. We've moved some of the greats. Abraham and Sarah used us when they came into the Land, and you know how fussy Sarah was. You be king, and leave the moving to us.

Advisor: We'll be going over a threshing floor. You'll have to watch out for bumps and holes.

Ahio: Don't worry. We've seen a few threshing floors in our day.

Advisor: What if the ox stumbles?

Uzza: The probability of that happening is virtually zero.

Advisor: But what would you do?

Uzza: No problem. I'd take a hold of the Ark and keep it in place. Pumping iron is part of our training as professional movers. Let's go.

Ahio: Oops, there goes the ox. Oh, no, there goes the Ark. Oh, no, there goes Uzza.

Advisor: Uzza has been struck down by God! I thought you guys said you knew what you were doing.

Ahio: I didn't say that. He said that. We'll never get our insurance renewed now.

David: Let's review what has happened. The cart carrying the Ark is stuck in a threshing floor. Uzza has been struck down by God. There is an ox with whiplash. This is not a good beginning.

Ahio: Nevertheless, Holy Ark Moving and Storage has a job to do and we'll do it. We'll deliver the Ark to your house in Jerusalem.

David: Does that delivery slip have *my* address on it? That's not right. I actually want it delivered to Obed-edom the Gittite.

Advisor: Sire, it is supposed to be housed at your palace.

David: The Holy Ark has great power. After what happened to Uzza, I'm not sure I want it anywhere near our workplace.

Advisor: Good point. Let's get the Ark over to Obed-edom's house.

* * *

Woman 1: Its the biggest parade to hit this land since Joshua crossed the Jordan. I had a hard time getting these seats.

Man: It's sure taken a long time to get this parade off the ground. It was scheduled for three months ago. Do you remember that?

Woman 2: Of course. We lined the streets to the king's palace waiting to greet the Holy Ark when the cart took a detour to Obed-edom's house. And what's a parade without floats?

Man: Evidently, God blessed Obed-edom because of the Ark and so the king has now decided that it was safe to bring it into the palace. Here they come.

Woman 1: I like the way King David made the sacrifice. Ooh! The Ark bearers are on the move again. Darn, I can't see anything now. There are too many people.

Man: Wait a minute, there's King David. He's dancing in front of the Ark. He's whirling and leaping and having a good old time.

Woman 1: I wish I could see. What's he wearing?

Man: Just a linen apron . . . a scanty linen apron. With nothing underneath! And he's leaping.

Woman 1: Everybody, get out of the way. I have a knife and I'm prepared to use it. I want a clear view of the parade or things will get ugly.

Woman 2: This is definitely the best parade I've ever attended. His wife, Michal, must have steam coming out of her ears.

Woman 1: Gasp! You're right, Michal must really be embarrassed.

Man: Why would you say that?

Woman 1: Michal is such a proper princess. Let's move in closer. There is bound to be some good action now.

Man: It's sad to see the day end. The Ark of God has come to rest in the tent that David pitched. It was a nice touch to have David bless the people and send us home with cakes. What are you two doing?

Woman 2: Shhh. We're standing in front of David's tent. Michal is coming out and she is furious. Listen.

David: Michal, darling. Why didn't you come to the parade? It was wonderful.

Michal: Wonderful? The king of Israel exposing himself to his subjects and slave girls is wonderful? You dishonored yourself.

David: Then I will dishonor myself even more, because God anointed me king and I intend to dance before God again and again.

Women: Hooray for the king. Let's have another parade tomorrow!

ETERNAL KINGSHIP
II Samuel 7:1-29

Narrator: When the king was settled in his palace and God had granted him safety from all his enemies, David called upon the prophet Nathan.

David: Nathan, I have a problem.

Nathan: Speak freely. Your sixty minutes are beginning . . . now.

David: I feel bad that I live in a house of cedar while the Ark of the Lord is in a tent.

Nathan: It's good that you're able to share these feelings.

David: What should I do?

Nathan: What would you like to do?

David: I want to build a Temple.

Nathan: You say you want to build a Temple. Then go with your feelings.

David: Are you sure . . . ?

Nathan: Time's up. We'll meet again tomorrow. I think we made excellent progress in this session.

God: Nathan, we have to talk.

Nathan: Speak freely. Your sixty minutes . . . oops, sorry. It's a force of habit.

God: You must tell David that he shall not be the one to build a Temple in which to house the Ark.

Nathan: Better I should have been an accountant.

David: Nathan, you've arrived earlier than expected. Come meet the architects and designers.

Nathan: David, we need to talk. I have some good news and some bad news.

David: I'll take the bad news first.

Nathan: God spoke to me.

David: Great! Did God like my dancing?

Nathan: We didn't discuss the arts. God told me that no one was ever asked to build a permanent Temple for the Ark before.

David: Then this must be a pleasant surprise. Do you think black is a good color for the curtain?

Designer: How about silver doorknobs?

Nathan: Furthermore, God has promised to make your kingdom powerful and you shall be known as one of the greatest men on earth.

Designer: Maybe the doorknobs should be gold.

David: Go on, Nathan. I'm beginning to like this.

Nathan: Israel will become secure and your kingship will be established forever. You will never lose favor as Saul did. There might be punishment for wrongdoing, but your throne will be eternal.

David: Great! Thanks for the chat. It was positively inspirational.

Nathan: Oh, and one thing more. One of your sons will be guided to build a Temple to God. Isn't that also great?

David: Did you say one of my sons? As in . . . not me?

Nathan: Don't get upset. Breathe slowly. Now, share your feelings. Don't hold back. Release your emotions. That's good.

David: I can't be upset. God has fullfilled a promise to establish my throne forever. There is none like the God of Israel, that's for sure. Besides, I'm happy that one of my children will be the one to build the Temple. I'm happy. I really am.

Nathan: That was wonderful. You've come a long way.

Designer: Now, what do we do with the ceramic birds I showed you?

David: Have them for lunch, for all I care.

Nathan: Let's discuss this little frustration in our Thursday group session.

THE EMPIRE IS BORN
II Samuel 8:1-10:19

Narrator: The Israelite armies, under King David, marched forth against the Philistines, the Moabites, the Edomites, and the Arameans. Each nation fell before the power of King David and Israel became an empire.

Israelite 1: Uh, oh. Here comes King Toi of Hamath.

David: Greetings, King Toi. Have you come to challenge Israel in battle?

Toi: Sure. I'm going to fight the mighty David who has already defeated Moab, Edom, Zobah, and Philistia, and who has annihilated the powerful Arameans. Do I look stupid?

David: Why are you here, then?

Toi: First of all, I want to congratulate you on your victory over Zobah. We were at war with them ourselves, so I guess you can say that we're your allies.

David: But we did all the fighting.

Toi: And you did a wonderful job. To show you our appreciation, I bring you gifts of gold, silver, and copper which you can dedicate to God.

David: Why do I get the feeling that you're trying to get on my good side?

Toi: Because I have a bit of wise philosophy that my father taught me. He said, "Son, always be friends with the biggest kid in the class."

David: With foreign affairs in order, I guess I had better take a look at the domestic front. I can see why Saul went crazy. There is so much to do.

Ziba: You summoned me. How can I be of service?

David: Yes, you were a servant of the House of Saul. Is that correct?

Ziba: That depends.

David: On what?

Ziba: Do you resent the House of Saul for the civil war that you had to fight in order to become king?

David: It's all in the past.

Ziba: Then the answer is yes. I was a servant of the House of Saul.

David: Off with his head.

Ziba: Oh, no!

David: Just kidding. I want to keep a promise that I made to Saul and Jonathan to protect their children. Are any of them left?

Ziba: Yes. There is Mephibosheth, the crippled son of Jonathan. He lives in Lo-debar.

David: Have him brought to me.

Mephibosheth: You summoned this humble, trembling servant?

David: Are you not the son of Jonathan and grandson of Saul?

Mephibosheth: That depends.

David: Let's not start this again. I'm not going to hurt you.

Mephibosheth: Yes, I am Mephibosheth of the House of Saul.

David: Cut off his hands.

Mephibosheth: My end has come.

Ziba: Naah. The king is quite a kidder. He's here to help you. But I have to warn you about something.

Mephibosheth: Like what?

Ziba: He has an electric buzzer in his hand. When he shakes your hand you'll get an electric shock. Just laugh along with him.

David: Mephibosheth, I want to keep faith with you for the sake of your father Jonathan. I am giving you back all of your grandfather Saul's land and you shall always eat at my table.

Mephibosheth: Is this a joke? I can't believe you'd do this for me.

David: I am quite serious. In addition, Ziba and his family and servants shall farm the land and serve you.

Ziba: Pretty funny. I love your sense of humor.

David: I'm not joking.

Mephibosheth: Ha, ha, ha.

David: Let's shake on it, Mephibosheth. Bzzzzz.

* * *

Joab: David, the Ammonites are gathering against us. They have hired Arameans to fight as well.

David: Don't these people ever learn? General Joab, I have a good mind to give them such a tongue lashing . . . .

Joab: Sire, I believe swords would be more effective.

David: Oh well, a leader's work is never done.

Narrator: In a great battle, the Arameans were totally destroyed by King David and Joab. The kings in the region all submitted to David whose empire continued to grow. And the Arameans decided that the Ammonites could fight their own battles in the future.

DAVID AND BATHSHEBA
II Samuel 11:1-27

Sonya: Mendel, hurry up. The show is going to start in a few minutes.

Mendel: Here's the popcorn, my little couch potato. Gertie, get the goats out of the kitchen so we can hear.

Sonya: Quiet! It's on.

Announcer: Welcome to Israel's most popular daytime and nighttime drama, "These Are the Days of David's Life." Here are some scenes from last week's episode.

David: Who is that woman bathing on the rooftop? She's beautiful.

Servant: That's Bathsheba, daughter of Eliam and wife of Uriah the Hittite.

David: Fetch her.

Servant: She's married.

David: I'm king.

Servant: Good point.

Announcer: Later that day, Bathsheba appears before David.

David: I want you for my own.

Bathsheba: I am a married woman.

David: I find you very beautiful. Kiss me.

Bathsheba: You're very handsome yourself, but I have a husband.

David: I'm king.

Bathsheba: Good point.

Announcer: Later, Bathsheba discovers she is pregnant. David calls Uriah home from the battlefield.

David: How are things at the front?

Uriah: The fighting is fierce. How are things at home?

David: Dull, very dull. You are such a good soldier that I wanted you to come home for a rest. Go to your wife and relax.

Announcer: But Uriah refused to go home, because he felt that he could not enjoy himself while his fellow comrades were in battle.

David: I can't understand this guy. Last night, I got Uriah drunk and he still wouldn't go home to his wife.

Announcer: We concluded last week's episode with Uriah refusing to go home, his wife pregnant, and David scratching his head for a way out of this dilemma. In a moment, today's program begins.

Sonya: What will the king do?

Mendel: It's obvious. He's gotta bump off Uriah. These soaps are so predictable.

Sonya: Why do you watch them?

Mendel: Did you see Bathsheba bathing on the roof?

Sonya: You're married!

Mendel: So's Bathsheba. *Quiet,* the show's starting.

David: Scribe, take a memo. This is to Joab on the battlefield. "I want Uriah placed on the front line where the fighting is the the most fierce."

Scribe: But, your majesty — Uriah could get killed.

David: Keep writing. "Then fall back so Uriah will be killed."

Scribe: That's terrible. How could you do that?

David: I'm king.

Scribe: Good point.

Mendel: I told you this would happen.

Sonya: I'm amazed. I've never seen this side of David.

Soldier: I have news from Joab about the battle.

David: What happened?

Soldier: The Ammonite city was under siege, but the enemy attacked and some of our officers fell.

David: Why did you get so close to the city? Didn't you know that they would shoot from the wall? What kind of thinking would bring you to this?

Soldier: Uriah was among those killed.

David: Oh, well, you win some, you lose some.

Soldier: You seem almost happy.

David: Nervous laughter. Tell Joab not to worry about the minor setback. Accidents do happen. Encourage him to attack the city and destroy it. Messenger, send for Bathsheba . . . the widow.

Bathsheba: You summoned me, your majesty?

David: I hear you have finished the mourning period for your late husband. It was terrible what happened to him. Kiss me.

Bathsheba: But I'm a new widow.

David: I'm king.

Bathsheba: Good point.

David: I want you to marry me.

Bathsheba: No, no, no. Yes, yes, yes.

David: Finally, you shall be my wife.

Bathsheba: I hope they have wedding gowns in my size.

Announcer: And now for some scenes from next week's show.

David: Bathsheba, you've given birth to a son.

Bathsheba: Yippee.

Announcer: Until next time, "These Are the Days of David's Life."

Sonya: That was wonderful. Mendel, you're crying.

Mendel: David has all the luck.

NATHAN'S PARABLE
II Samuel 12:1-25

Narrator: God was displeased with what David had done concerning Bathsheba and Uriah and sent the prophet Nathan to David.

David: Greetings, Nathan. It's always great to see you.

Nathan: Today I come to you with a parable.

David: I love stories. Is this one of those fables with a hidden message? I love trying to guess the meaning.

Nathan: Once upon a time there was a rich man.

Rich Man: I am so rich. I've got large flocks and herds. I've got so much money.

Nathan: And there was a poor man in the same city.

Poor Man: I'm so poor. I just have this little lamb. I've tended it and fed it. It's like a child to me.

David: This is so touching. I like the poor guy a lot. I was once a shepherd.

Nathan: Such a coincidence. One day, a traveler came as a guest to the rich man's house.

Rich Man: I'm not wasting any animals from my flock on this stranger.

Nathan: And so he took the little lamb that the poor man loved like a child to cook for the stranger's dinner.

Poor Man: Good-bye, my little friend.

Lamb: Don't let the mean, rich man take me.

Poor Man: I have no choice.

Rich Man: Let's go. Dinner is at six.

Lamb: Bah, bah. Dah, dah.

Poor Man: My baby.

David: Stop, I can't take it anymore. That poor, poor man. The rich man is heartless and deserves to die. He shall pay fourfold for the lamb because he showed no pity. I demand to see that evil person right now.

Nathan: You are that man.

David: No way. I don't even like lamb.

Nathan: David, this is a parable. God is angry with you. You were anointed king over Israel and Judah. God rescued you from Saul. You have been given an empire. Which character in the parable does that make you?

David: Not the lamb.

Nathan: You took poor Uriah's wife and then arranged for him to be killed.

David: You make it sound so terrible. I'm sure the rich man had some positive qualities and had good intentions.

Lamb: Bah, bah. Dah, dah.

Poor Man: My baby.

David: Okay, I'm guilty. Punish me. Anything. Just let the lamb go.

Nathan: God will cause an uprising from within your house. Your wives will be taken from you. Your dirty deeds were done in secret. The punishment shall be done in broad daylight.

David: I said I was sorry.

Nathan: Your admission of guilt is accepted. You shall not die, but Bathsheba's son will.

Bathsheba: David, our son is afflicted with a terrible illness.

David: Ooo, that was fast.

Narrator: David prayed and fasted for the boy, but on the seventh day the infant died. David then rose, bathed, and ate.

Servant: Your majesty, we don't understand. While your baby was ill, you wouldn't eat or sleep. But when your child died, you rose up and took food.

David: I thought maybe God would have pity on me and the child would live. But now that the baby has died, it's time to get on with my life.

Narrator: And David went to his wife and consoled her. Bathsheba bore another son and she named him Solomon.

SCANDAL IN THE PALACE
II Samuel 13:1-39

Secretary: The editorial board of the *National Sin-quirer* is now in session.

Editor: Let's go over the story possibilities for this week.

Reporter 1: We'd like to lead off with the lady in Asher giving birth to a two-headed elephant.

Editor: That's good, but we need something that will grab people's attention. Nobody cares about elephants.

Reporter 2: How about a follow-up to the David and Bathsheba story?

Editor: We've been milking that story for fifteen years. We need a new palace scandal.

Reporter 3: I've been covering the Absalom beat, and I think I have a lead.

Editor: Not another story about the spoiled good-looking prince.

Reporter 3: No! As word has it, Absalom is really angry at his half-brother Amnon. It seems that Amnon has a crush on Absalom's sister Tamar.

Editor: David has certainly raised some wonderful children.

Reporter 1: We could call the story "Puppy Love in the Palace."

Reporter 3: There's more! Amnon faked being sick and requested that Tamar serve him food.

Secretary: Ooh. This is really getting juicy. I didn't think Amnon was that smart. I still remember the story we did on Amnon when he failed kindergarten three times.

Reporter 3: Actually, the idea came from his first cousin and pal, Yonadab. Anyhow, Tamar comes to the sick bed of Amnon and the guy grabs her.

Reporter 2: We could call the story "Passion in the Palace."

Reporter 3: Here's the clincher. After that incident, Amnon decided that he didn't like Tamar anymore. So he kicked her out of his room. She was really upset and ran to her brother Absalom. She's at his house now.

Reporter 2: We can call the story "Pity in the Palace."

Editor: I'll bet David is very upset about this.

Reporter 3: He's been on bicarbonates for a week.

Editor: Let's go with this story of passion as our cover feature.

Secretary: I really liked the two-headed elephant story better.

* * *

Narrator: Two years after the Amnon incident, Absalom was having his sheep sheared and he invited all of his father's sons to join him. David declined to go himself, but he sent Amnon with all the other princes.

Amnon: Absalom, it was really nice of you to invite me to this festive occasion.

Absalom: We're brothers, aren't we?

Amnon: I thought you might still be sore about what happened with Tamar.

186

Absalom: There's no point in holding a grudge, brother dear. After all, Tamar is happy staying at my house, crying in her room. Have some more wine.

Servant: Absalom, you called me.

Absalom: See to it that Amnon has plenty to drink.

Servant: It's amazing how you are willing to treat him so well after what he did. I read the story in the *National Sin-quirer*. You are really a saint for forgiving him like this.

Absalom: When he is drunk, have him killed.

Servant: Well, you're an evil saint.

Absalom: And then pack me a mule. I have a feeling that Dad is not going to be too happy with me. I'll be staying with the King of Geshur.

* * *

Narrator: Let's look in on the staff of the *National Sin-quirer* three years later. They are meeting to discuss current lawsuits.

Editor: Let's review the lawsuits that are pending.

Reporter 1: King David is still suing us for that story we ran three years ago.

Editor: Which one?

Reporter 2: Remember, Absalom had Amnon killed at the shearing party. But we reported that Absalom had also killed every other son of the king.

Reporter 1: King David heard the rumor that all of his sons were dead and, needless to say, he was a little depressed.

Editor: Our story wasn't true, was it?

187

Reporter 3: But it made for a much juicier story the way we told it.

Secretary: I understand that King David has gotten over Amnon's death and now wants his precious Absalom to come home.

Editor: Let's be thankful that the king doesn't run the country like he runs his family. Are there any other lawsuits?

Secretary: Yes. The lady who had the two-headed elephant is suing us, because we ran the story before she had a chance to tell her husband.

ABSALOM RETURNS HOME

II Samuel 14:1-33

Joab: King David, how are things today?

David: I don't know.

Joab: What are you doing?

David: I'm watching the dust settle on the window sill.

Joab: I hate to tear you away from that important task. However, there is a woman here to see you.

David: Very well, Joab, show her in.

Joab: Remember, you have to make this seem real.

Woman: Hey, I'm the best actress in Judah. I can play any part with my eyes closed. This will be a piece of cake.

Joab: The king is completely preoccupied with his son Absalom. He misses him terribly.

Woman: I have no idea why. Absalom is stuck on himself. And then, there was that little thing about killing his brother Amnon.

Joab: Nevertheless, the king will not be happy until his son returns. The trick is getting him to realize it. There's the king now.

Woman: I've always wondered what kings do every day. What's David up to?

Joab: He's watching the dust settle on the window sill.

Woman: Life is tough at the top.

Joab: Your majesty, I bring you a woman from Tekoa who bears a petition.

Woman: Woe is me. Woe, woe. Oy, oy, oy. Help me king. I throw myself at your feet. I grieve for my husband. Woe, woe, woe.

David: You seem upset about something.

Woman: My husband died and we had two sons. The sons had a fight in the field and it came to blows. One killed the other. Everybody wants to put my remaining son to death. If he dies, there will be no heir and my husband will be without a son to carry on his name.

David: That's terrible. What do you think, Joab?

Joab: I think she's very good. I mean, very good at making her point.

David: Go home, and I'll issue an edict on your behalf. Not a hair on your son's head shall be harmed.

Woman: May I say one more thing.

David: Of course.

Woman: If you would agree that my son and I not be cut off from our inheritance, why won't you bring back your own son? You are condemning yourself in not doing so. I know that I am just a handmaiden, but you are a like an angel of God and you understand so much.

David: Answer me this. Does Joab have anything to do with your being here?

Woman: Uh, oh.

David: Don't hold anything back. Remember that I'm the guy who slew Goliath. Would you like to see how I did that?

Woman: When you put it that way . . . Joab was the one who told me what to say. I am just a simple actress from Tekoa.

David: That's right. I remember you. You were wonderful in "Camel on a Hot Cloth Tent." Joab, what do you have to say for yourself?

Joab: I thought she was very good in that show.

David: All right, I'll do it. Bring back my boy Absalom. There is one condition. He is not to present himself to me.

Narrator: Joab went at once to Geshur to bring Absalom back to Jerusalem.

Servant: I'm going to get a hernia from this job.

Joab: What is going on here?

Servant: Absalom is getting his annual haircut.

Joab: You mean, all that hair in your wheelbarrow is from Absalom?

Servant: Yes, and two other loads as well. He cuts it once a year when it grows too heavy for his head. Did you know that his hair weighs two hundred shekels?

Joab: Yes, I read about it in the *National Sin-quirer.*

Servant: Absalom is in the tent.

Joab: Absalom, it is Joab.

Absalom: Let me take a look in the mirror. Wow, I am as handsome as they say I am.

Joab: I'm here to bring you back to Jerusalem.

Absalom: Dad finally gave in! When do I see him?

Joab: As they say at the dry cleaners, patience is a virtue.

Narrator: Absalom returned and lived in Jerusalem for two years without appearing before the king.

Servant 2: Absalom, I have returned from Joab, but the general won't come.

Absalom: That's the second time I have asked to see him.

Servant 2: Maybe he's avoiding you.

Absalom: Maybe he's avoiding me. Of course, he is. I've got to get his attention. That field next to ours belongs to the general, right?

Servant 2: He grows barley there.

Absalom: Oops. I set a fire. Oh, how clumsy of me. It seems to be spreading to Joab's field.

Servant 2: Should I get water?

Absalom: No thanks, I'm not thirsty.

Servant 2: Uh, oh, here comes Joab.

Joab: Absalom, why did you set my fields on fire?

Absalom: I wanted your attention and it seems to have worked. I want to see my father. If he puts me to death, that's fine. Otherwise, I should have stayed in Geshur.

Joab: I get the point. But there must be a less expensive way to send a message.

Narrator: Joab reported what Absalom had said to King David and the king summoned him. Absalom flung himself to the ground before his father. King David kissed Absalom and forgave him.

Absalom: Hey, Dad, don't muss the hair.

ABSALOM'S REVOLT

II Samuel 15:1-16:23

Announcer: Good evening, ladies and gentlemen. We interrupt "The Zebulun Hillbillies" for a special report. We are going live to Hebron for an important announcement. Absalom, son of David, has called a press conference and should be appearing shortly. Now, over to Moshe Wallinsky.

Moshe: Thank you. It's a balmy evening in Hebron and a multitude of Absalom's supporters have gathered here for an important message from their leader. As you know, Absalom has been gaining tremendous popularity over the years.

Announcer: Moshe, some say that the king's son has been acting as if he was running for the throne. He has spent a lot of time by the city gates greeting people and talking about how he would dispense justice.

Moshe: There is talk that Absalom is going to throw his crown into the race. Let's see. The prince is ready to begin.

Secretary: Good evening, Israel and Judah. Tonight, we have the opportunity to hear from a great man. I present to you the next king of Israel — Absalom, son of David.

Moshe: The crowd is going crazy!

Absalom: Thank you, my subjects. As you know, David has been king for a long time. But this is a new generation and we need fresh ideas.

Secretary: Everybody together — "Run, Absalom, run."

Absalom: I'd like to introduce my father's former chief counselor, Ahithopel, who has joined the ticket. The tide has turned. Victory is almost ours.

Announcer: There you have it. Absalom has claimed the throne and is in open rebellion. We now go for a report to the palace of King David with Batya Wasser.

Batya: Hello. Hello. There is a feeling of emptiness at the palace.

Announcer: Why is that?

Batya: Well, for one thing, the palace is empty. David and his court have left the city. It was a very sad sight. People were crying and sobbing all over the place.

Announcer: What about the Ark of God? Did he take that with him?

Batya: Yes and no. The Levites took it with them, but David sent it back for safety reasons.

Announcer: Did anyone stay behind?

Batya: Oddly enough, David's close advisor, Hushai, stayed in town. Rumor has it that he is defecting to Absalom. Earlier in the day, we taped an interview with King David.

David: Hello, Batya.

Batya: King, how do you feel about what your son Absalom is saying?

David: I have heard his comments and my only question is, "Where's the Beef"? He talks of new ideas, but I don't see them being put into practice.

Announcer: Thank you, Batya for a wonderful interview. We have a late breaking report from the field.

Fruma: This is Fruma Bat Fruma, live on the road with King David and his party. It's been a day of ups and downs. Ziba, servant of Mephibosheth, Jonathan's son, brought out supplies for the troops. The entourage was then confronted by Shimei, a member of Saul's family. We have this on tape.

194

Shimei: You no good (bleep). Get out of here, you (bleep) of (bleep). God is paying you back for (bleep) the throne that you stole from my family.

Fruma: David, what is your response?

David: God is using Shimei to punish me. But his insults are nothing compared to my own son's rebellion. I must say, however, that some of his remarks have made even me blush. I had no idea that the Hebrew language could be so colorful.

Fruma: This is Fruma Bat Fruma live and exhausted from the camp of King David.

Announcer: To summarize the day, Absalom has now entered Jerusalem and was greeted by King David's former close advisor Hushai. Absalom seems to be in complete control. We now return you to "Menasheh Vice" already in progress.

THE END OF THE REVOLT

II Samuel 17:1-19:1

Absalom: We're definitely going to have to redo this palace. There aren't enough mirrors around.

Ahithopel: Sire.

Absalom: Who? Oh, me. It will take a while to get used to being addressed as the king.

Ahithopel: King Absalom.

Absalom: Okay, I've adjusted.

Ahithopel: Before you redecorate the palace, I think we need to finish off your father. Give me twelve thousand men. We should attack him while he is tired and weak. Then there will be complete peace.

Absalom: Sounds great. What color do you think would be best in the throne room?

Hushai: May I say something.

Absalom: Of course. Hushai, you were my father's most trusted advisor. Do you agree with Ahithopel's plan?

Hushai: Not at all. If you attack now, you'll be defeated. David is an experienced fighter and has courageous soldiers. I think you should wait and gather as many men as you can from all over Israel and then march against him.

Absalom: That sound like a better idea, Hushai. It guarantees me a success and gives me more time to plan the victory party.

Ahithopel: I can't believe that you would follow this traitor's advice. He betrayed his king.

Hushai: So did you.

Ahithopel: Did not.

Hushai: Did so.

Absalom: Knock it off. I'm taking Hushai's advice. Now can we get down to some serious discussion on color schemes for the carpet?

Ahithopel: Forget it. I'm obviously not needed here. I'm going home.

Hushai: Good riddance. Your majesty, I shall be right back. The priests Zadok and Abiathar are here to see me.

Zadok: Hushai, we came as soon as you called.

Hushai: Zadok, get word to David that he must move his troops across the river. I've just bought him some time.

Zadok: What's happening?

Hushai: As soon as Absalom finishes with his interior designer, he will cross the Jordan with a large force.

Narrator: King David gathered his thousands of troops to meet the army of Absalom.

David: I'm dressed and ready to go. Sound the shofar.

Joab: The troops will not allow you to go into battle. You must be protected. It'll be better for you to support us from the town.

David: All right, but go easy on my son Absalom. Do not harm him.

Joab: Oh, sure, when we run into him, we'll tell him he was a naughty boy and have him stand in the corner.

Soldier: Joab, the battle is going well. The followers of Absalom have been defeated in the forest of Ephraim.

Joab: Have you found Absalom?

Soldier: Yes.

Joab: He's not going to get away, is he?

Soldier: I doubt it. He was riding his mule under a tree and his hair got caught. The mule kept going, but Absalom didn't.

Absalom: Get me down from here.

Joab: Hello, Absalom. What are you doing? Hanging out?

Absalom: Ha, ha, ha.

Joab: Kill the brat.

Soldier: You heard what David said. I wouldn't touch him for a thousand shekels.

Absalom: Tough luck, Joab. My father still loves me and he'll forgive me for my slight indiscretion.

Joab: Slight? You killed his son. You led a rebellion. You forced him out of Jerusalem. And to top it off, you sent an army against him.

Absalom: He'll probably cut my allowance.

Joab: You need some old fashioned disciplining.

Absalom: What are you going to do? Spank me and send me to my room?

Joab: I thought I'd play darts with you as my target.

Absalom: You wouldn't dare.

Joab: Bull's eye.

Narrator: Joab's men took Absalom and flung him into a large pit and covered it with stones. Then all the Israelites fled to their homes.

Sentry: Your majesty, two messengers are running.

David: Do they look happy or sad?

Sentry: They're wearing happy faces.

David: Good news, at last.

Messenger 1: Congratulations, all is well.

David: Is Absalom okay?

Messenger 2: It was a striking victory.

David: Is Absalom okay?

Messenger 2: May all your enemies meet his fate.

David: My son Absalom! Oh, my son, my son, Absalom.

Messenger 1: The king isn't taking this too well.

THE RETURN OF THE KING
II Samuel 19:2-20:22

David: Absalom, my Absalom.

Servant: If he doesn't stop with the "Absalom, my Absalom," he is going to drive us nuts.

Joab: What's going on here? This place should be celebrating, but it looks like we're at a funeral.

Servant: Perhaps, you should take off your party hat, general.

David: Absalom, my Absalom.

Joab: Your majesty, may I speak with you?

David: Absalom, my Absalom.

Joab: Pull yourself together. You're showing love for those who hate you and hate for those who love you. Knock it off.

David: Thanks, I needed that.

Joab: Now, go out there and tell the troops you love them. Take off that nasty pout. That's better. Give me a happy face. Put on this party hat and get the celebration going.

Narrator: David passed back over the Jordan with all the Judite soldiers and part of the Israelite army on his return to Jerusalem.

Israel: Hey, how come the tribe of Judah gets to march next to David?

Judah: Because he is from our tribe.

Israel: That's not fair.

Judah: That's politics.

Sheba: Gather to me, House of Israel. We have no portion in David. Prepare for war.

David: What is happening?

Joab: Sheba the Benjaminite is stirring things up. It looks like we have another rebellion on our hands.

David: Good grief. I haven't even unpacked from the last one.

Joab: We have Sheba's men cornered in the city of Abel.

David: Good, I'm tired of living out of a suitcase.

Narrator: All of the troops of Joab were engaged in battering the walls where Sheba was.

Woman: Psst. Joab, may I have a word with you?

Joab: Certainly.

Woman: Do I look like a reasonable person?

Joab: Yes.

Woman: Then, let me share my thoughts with you. Are you cuckoo? You're going to destroy one of the oldest cities in the land.

Joab: Hey, I don't want to burn this town. I just want to get my hands on that scoundrel Sheba who is trying to stir up trouble.

Woman: No Sheba, no trouble?

Joab: That's right.

Woman: Don't move from this spot. Leave everything to me.

Joab: I'll be waiting with bells on.

Woman: People of Abel. I have found a way to save our town.

Townsman: Hooray. What military strategy have you found?

Sheba: I certainly welcome your help.

Woman: I was hoping you'd say that. If we turn Sheba over to Joab, the town is saved.

Sheba: Are you mad? We are at the forefront of a great revolution. Victory is at hand.

Woman: Really? I see a few of your guys on the wall and thousands of Joab's troops battering our walls down.

Sheba: We can win.

Woman: You're living in fantasy land. Those are real spears and swords out there.

Townsman: What are the choices?

Woman: We could support Sheba and all die painful deaths, or we could turn him over to Joab and live. It's a tough decision. Shall we distribute ballots?

Townsman: Gee, I just don't know how I'm going to vote. Life or death. Let me think.

Soldier: Joab, I think the revolution is over.

Joab: Why do you say that?

Soldier: They just threw Sheba's body over the wall.

Joab: That could definitely signal the end of his revolt.

Narrator: Joab sounded the horn and all the troops dispersed to their homes. The general returned to King David in Jerusalem.

A CENSUS IS TAKEN

II Samuel 24:1-25

Clerk: Knock, knock.

Asher: Come in. The door is open.

Clerk: Thank goodness. You are the last house I have to cover and then I can go back to Jerusalem.

Asher: Are you from the government?

Clerk: Yes, we're taking a census of men eligible for the draft.

Mrs. Asher: This is awful. God commanded that no census ever be taken among our people.

Clerk: So, write your congressperson. Can I get on with my job? I'm not being paid by the hour.

Asher: The prophet Samuel warned us that this would happen if we anointed a king.

Clerk: Hey, enough complaining. How many eligible men are there here?

Mrs. Asher: Counting my husband, there are four.

Clerk: Thank you. What are you watching?

Asher: Just the news. David reburied Saul and Jonathan and he wrote a song about Saul's life.

Clerk: Is it any good?

Mrs. Asher: I'm sure it'll go gold. He could have been quite a singing star, but he gave it all up to be king. Who can figure?

Asher: Oh, yeah. They've announced that David will no longer be going out into battle. The Philistines almost got him.

Clerk: That's going to go over real well with the anti-draft people.

* * *

Gad: David, it's a pleasure to see you.

David: I have sinned before God. I should not have taken a census. I'm prepared to take my punishment.

Gad: That's a coincidence, because God has sent me here to deliver a punishment.

David: What should I do?

Gad: Pick a card. Any card.

David: What?

Gad: Well, you're being given a choice of three punishments. Would you like a seven year famine?

Advisor: No, not another famine. Everyone hates famines.

David: What's the next choice?

Gad: You would be put to flight and your enemies would pursue you for three months.

David: I'm too old for that kind of stuff.

Advisor: Good, I hate packing and traveling.

David: What else do you have?

Gad: We could give you three days of pestilence.

204

David: That's all the choices? What ever happened to being grounded or no telephone privileges? I can't choose. I'll leave it up to God.

Gad: Then prepare yourself for pestilence.

David: Order 2,000 cans of bug spray.

Advisor: David, you must do something. Over 70,000 people have perished in this plague.

David: I will build an altar and pray to God to stop this plague.

Narrator: David built an altar and sacrificed offerings of well-being. And God responded by halting the plague in the land.

SOLOMON IS CHOSEN
I Kings 1:1-53

Narrator: As King David grew close to death, his son Adonijah went about boasting that he would be crowned king.

Servant: Prince Adonijah, did you call me?

Adonijah: I am so excited. Do you know what today is?

Servant: I hope we didn't forget your birthday.

Adonijah: Even better.

Servant: I hope we didn't forget my birthday.

Adonijah: Today is one day closer to when I will be king.

Servant: I'll go make a cake.

Joab: Adonijah, may we come in?

Adonijah: Of course. Hello, Joab and Abiathar, my two most trusted allies.

Abiathar: You seem to be in a good mood.

Adonijah: Father gets older by the day.

Servant: Your highly perceptive mind continues to impress your humble servant.

Adonijah: Do you know that they brought in Abishag the Shunamite to warm his bed? But Pop is so old that he ignored her. And, as we all know, that Shunamite is dynamite.

Joab: I hope you aren't jumping the gun.

Adonijah: I'm not. I was next in line after Absalom and just as good looking. Since Absalom is no longer with us, that makes me the crown prince. Who can dispute my claim?

Abiathar: Let me see. There's Bathsheba, the priest Zadok, Benaiah, the prophet Nathan . . . and, of course, your brother Solomon.

Adonijah: So there are a couple of other contenders. Big deal.

Abiathar: Not to mention David's inner circle of fighting men.

Adonijah: You certainly know how to spoil a festive mood.

Joab: If you want to be king, we have to make our move now.

Adonijah: I'm one step ahead of you. Are the invitations ready?

Servant: Ta da. Three hundred invitations to the Coronation Ball of Adonijah. I personally calligraphed them. Each one took an hour.

Adonijah: Let me see them. Oops, I forgot to tell you. I've decided not to invite Solomon, Nathan, Benaiah, and these ten others.

Servant: There goes fifteen hours of hard work. The next time you want invitations, get hired help to do it.

Adonijah: You are hired help.

Servant: Oh.

* * *

Nathan: Bathsheba, did you hear about Adonijah?

207

Bathsheba: What is that egomaniac up to?

Nathan: That egomaniac is claiming the throne without David's knowledge.

Bathsheba: I'll be suprised if they can find a crown big enough for his head.

Nathan: If Adonijah becomes king, you know what will happen to you and your son.

Bathsheba: Yes. We'll be chopped liver.

Nathan: You've got to tell David what Adonijah is doing, and then I'll conveniently enter and confirm your words.

Bathsheba: That's sneaky.

Nathan: It might save the throne for your son, Solomon.

Bathsheba: I'm on my way.

David: Bathsheba, it's a pleasure to see you. What troubles you?

Bathsheba: I thought you were dead.

David: That's news to me.

Bathsheba: You didn't receive an invitation to the party either. Adonijah has declared himself king and is celebrating right now. I thought you must have died.

David: I can't believe it. He's having a party and didn't invite his old man.

Bathsheba: Do you realize what will happen to me and Solomon if Adonijah becomes king?

David: Sure. You're chopped liver.

Nathan: David, I thought you were dead.

David: I wish people would stop saying that.

Nathan: Hello, Bathsheba. What a suprise it is to see you!

Bathsheba: Why, Nathan, it's been centuries.

Nathan: David, Adonijah is calling himself king and is having a party. I wasn't even invited. Neither was Zadok nor Benaiah nor Solomon.

David: This is an outrage. Having a party without me is bad enough, but the fun of being king is getting to announce your successor. Bathsheba, I promised the throne to your son Solomon. He shall be king, as I swore. Let's take care of it now.

Bathsheba: May my lord King David live forever.

David: Oh, good, I'm alive again. Summon Zadok the priest, Benaiah, and all my loyal soldiers. Take Solomon to Gihon on my mule and have him anointed king there. Let's show Adonijah how a real party is thrown.

* * *

Adonijah: Let's bring on the dancing Phoenicians. It's party time.

Guest 1: It sounds like the real party is going on outside.

Guest 2: Listen to the noise. Check it out. There are flute players and horns and the people are going wild.

Adonijah: I want to know who is having a party at the same time as mine. That's incredibly rude.

Jonathan: Adonijah, I have just come from the streets.

Adonijah: Jonathan, my friend, what is going on?

Jonathan: David has made Solomon king. Nathan and Zadok anointed him at Gihon, and Solomon is at this moment sitting on the throne. The king's courtiers have blessed him, and David is said to be very happy. The whole town is celebrating.

Guest 1: I think we'll be going now.

Guest 2: Thanks for the quiche.

Servant: All right, everyone, we're ready to serve the roast cow. Hey, where did everyone go?

Joab: The party's over.

Servant: Oh, great. I worked very hard on this meal. I even stuffed an apple in the cow's mouth.

Joab: Adonijah, what are you going to do?

Adonijah: I'm going to the tent where the Ark is and beg for a pledge that Solomon will not kill me.

Servant: Adonijah, stop crying.

Adonijah: My brother has been anointed king. He will want to eliminate me. I assumed kingship prematurely which means that Dad will not be very supportive. I have no future, no friends, and no luck. It's my party and I'll cry if I want to.

Servant: This means that you won't be king. This is just great. I'm going over to the palace and see if I can get my old job back.

Adonijah: You would cry, too, if it happened to you.

Narrator: Solomon swore that if Adonijah behaved properly, nothing would happen to him. Adonijah was taken from the tent of the Ark and was sent home.

Servant: Good riddance and don't expect me to calligraph your change of business cards.

SOLOMON CONSOLIDATES POWER

I Kings 2:1-46

David: Solomon, my son, pretty soon I will be gone. You will be in charge of walking in God's ways and following the laws. You'll take over The Family and all of our businesses.

Solomon: Don't talk like this, poppa. You sound like you're getting ready to die.

David: The time is coming. Remember to keep the teachings of Moses and Adonai will keep all the promises made to our family. God is an important ally. If God makes an offer, don't refuse. Capische?

Solomon: Capische, poppa.

David: We have some plans to make. What will you do about Joab? He's been my general for years, but he killed some good men like Abner. He shouldn't rest in peace.

Solomon: He'll be dealt with. We'll take permanent care of him.

David: You must also deal with Shimei the Benjaminite. When we were hiding out during the family war with Absalom, he said some very insulting things about me. He begged forgiveness on my return, and I promised him that I would not put out a contract on him. It was out of respect for his family.

Solomon: But I didn't promise him anything.

David: You are a smart boy. You catch on real fast. You'll take good care of The Family. I've been godfather for forty years. I want to spend time with my grandchildren and work in the garden.

Solomon: Whatever you want, poppa. Pass the pasta.

Bathsheba: Solomon, what has happened?

Solomon: David is dead.

Bathsheba: May his name live forever.

Solomon: It will. I have a plan.

Bathsheba: Your brother Adonijah has come to ask for your father's handmaid Abishag.

Solomon: What a meatball. He wants to maneuver himself to become the head of The Family. It's time to go to work.

Benaiah: Solomon, we are ready.

Solomon: I want this to be smooth. I will be attending a nice quiet ceremony in town. I don't know nothing. Got it?

Benaiah: In twelve hours, your enemies will be wearing cement boots in a swimming pool.

Adonijah: Come in, the door is open.

Benaiah: I have a gift from Solomon.

Adonijah: A bowl of fortune cookies. How nice. I'll take one right now. It says,"Today is the last day of the rest of your life." I'll try another. "Yesterday was the next to the last day of the rest of your life."

Benaiah: Bye-bye.

Rocco: Is this the abode of Abiathar ?

Abiathar: Who are you?

Rocco: My name is Rocco and I bring a message from

Solomon to the former priest Abiathar.

Abiathar: What do you mean by "former" priest?

Rocco: You backed the wrong boy. You should pay with your life, but because you shared hardships with David, the boss has decided that you will be taking an early retirement.

Abiathar: Where are you sending me?

Rocco: Back to your hometown of Anathoth.

Abiathar: What if I refuse?

Rocco: Then I'll share a secret with you. I don't really have a violin in this violin case.

Abiathar: I'm packing.

Benaiah: Hello, Joab. The Family has a message for you.

Joab: I am holding onto the horns of the altar in the Tent of the Lord. I have sanctuary. You can't harm me while I am here.

Benaiah: That's right. You have nothing to be afraid of. Come outside.

Joab: No, I will die here.

Benaiah: As you wish.

Joab: You're going to break one of our sacred rules.

Benaiah: Joab, you broke a few rules when you killed innocent men.

Joab: You wouldn't dare.

Benaiah: That's what you think. A contract is a contract.

Solomon: How did everything go?

Benaiah: We took care of everybody. Real good care.

Rocco: What do we do now, boss?

Solomon: The Family will need some new blood. Benaiah, I am appointing you my right hand man. And Zadok will take over for Abiathar.

Rocco: There's only one loose end. How about Shimei the Benjaminite?

Solomon: I made a promise to Shimei that as long as he stays in Jerusalem, he will not come to harm. The moment he leaves the city, his blood will be on his own head.

Benaiah: We'll set up a stakeout.

Solomon: Good. I think that sometime in the future some slaves are going to happen to run away and he's going to go after them.

Rocco: And we nail him, right?

Solomon: Smart boy, Rocco.

Narrator: And two slaves ran away from Shimei. He chased after them and brought them home. Solomon called Shimei before him and reminded him of their oath. The king gave orders to Benaiah to strike the Benjaminite down. Thus the kingdom was secure in Solomon's hands.

SOLOMON THE WISE

I Kings 3:1-28

Priest: Solomon, it is a great honor to have you come to Gibeon to offer your sacrifices. And allow me to wish you *mazal tov* on your marriage to the daughter of the Pharaoh of Egypt.

Solomon: Thank you. Your open shrines were lovely. Now, I must rest.

Priest: Of course. But first, I need you to sign a few forms.

Solomon: For what?

Priest: Paper work. Nothing important. Sign here . . . and here. And over here, write "To little Chaim. Love, King Solomon."

Solomon: Now may I rest?

Priest: Absolutely. Oh, did I mention how delighted we are to have you worship here?

Solomon: Only about twenty times. Good night.

Priest: Quiet, everyone. My personal friend, King Solomon, would like some sleep. Oh, yes, he is a friend. He even signed an autograph for my son, Chaim. Shhh.

God: Solomon, it is Adonai. What shall I grant you?

Solomon: Deal kindly with me. I am still young and have no experience in leadership. How do I deal with all these people?

Priest: I said to keep it down. Maybe I can mention your problem to him later. The king, my close friend for many years, is sleeping right now.

Solomon: Oh, grant me the wisdom to deal with people. I have to be able to judge people correctly.

God: Because you didn't ask first for riches . . .

Solomon: Ooh. I forgot about that.

God: Nor did you ask for a long life. . .

Solomon: That also would have been nice.

God: You asked for wisdom. That you shall be given. And I shall also grant you what you didn't ask for. You shall have both riches and glory like none before you.

Solomon: Well, if You insist.

God: All I ask is that you follow in My ways and observe My laws as your father David did.

Priest: Hello, sleepyhead. It's time to rouse the royal body.

Solomon: I had a wondrous dream.

Priest: Why don't you tell me all about it?

Solomon: I must return to Jerusalem and offer sacrifices before the Ark of the Covenant. And then I shall hold a great banquet.

Priest: I'd be honored to attend. Hey, everyone. Solomon is returning to Jerusalem to throw a big party, and guess who is being invited?

* * *

Advisor: Welcome back to Jerusalem. How was Gibeon?

Solomon: Interesting. What's on today's agenda?

217

Advisor: You have an appointment with *Architecture Digest*. They want to do a story on the new palace and the walls around Jerusalem that you just completed.

Solomon: Who are these people coming in?

Advisor: Wardrobe and make-up. You're due on the set for "Solomon's Day Court."

Solomon: I didn't know we had a show today.

Advisor: The court is getting more and more popular. We've had to add an evening version. Your wisdom is quite a hit.

Dalia: This is Dalia Levin and welcome to "Solomon's Day Court." Our first case is about to begin. Let's meet the litigants.

Announcer: The plaintiff says that she gave birth to a son. Three days later, the defendant — who lives in the same house — also gave birth to a baby. Plaintiff claims that the defendant's child died, and that the defendant switched babies. Plaintiff is suing for custody of the living infant. The defendant claims that the baby is hers. We call this the "Case of the Breathing Baby."

Solomon: The court is now in session. My job is to determine who is the child's real mother. Let me hear from the plaintiff first.

Plaintiff: I gave birth to a son.

Solomon: Can you show the court who your son is?

Plaintiff: He's over there.

Defendant: He's my son. The dead boy is yours.

Plaintiff: The live one is mine. The dead boy is yours.

Solomon: Ladies. This is your first and last warning. No more outbreaks.

Plaintiff: My friend here gave birth to a boy three days after my son was born.

Solomon: Were there any witnesses?

Defendant: Nobody was around.

Plaintiff: The defendant lay on her child during her sleep and he died. When she realized what happened, she rose at night and switched babies. I arose to nurse and looked closely at the infant and realized it wasn't my son.

Solomon: How do you know it wasn't your son?

Plaintiff: To begin with, my child is the live one.

Defendant: My child is the live one. Yours is the dead one.

Plaintiff: Yours is the dead one.

Solomon: Order in the court. We've heard from the litigants. I'll be back in a moment with my decision.

Dalia: Which way do you think Solomon will rule? It's a tough call to make. Israel waits. Solomon is returning to the court again. All rise.

Solomon: Ladies, this is an interesting case. There are no witnesses. Neither of you has any proof. You both insist you are telling the truth. Therefore, I rule for both the defendant . . .

Defendant: I win. I win.

Solomon: . . . and I rule for the plaintiff.

Plaintiff: I win. I win.

Solomon: Bring the baby forward. This is what I call divided custody.

Defendant: You mean, we share the baby on different days?

Solomon: No, it means that I divide the child in two and give each of you custody of half.

Defendant: I want the top half.

Plaintiff: No! Give her the child! Don't kill him . . . don't hurt him!

Defendant: Oh, sure. Make me look like the villain. Go ahead, carry out your ruling. Cut him in two. I call "heads."

Solomon: Give the child to the plaintiff. She is the real mother. She would give it up, rather than see it die.

Dalia: Let's talk to the litigants as they leave the courtroom. You must be very happy with the decision.

Plaintiff: Yes! I have my baby back. Solomon is as wise as they say.

Dalia: Thank you. Step over there, the bailiff has some papers for you to sign. Here comes the defendant. What you did was really awful.

Defendant: Hey, it was dark. It was an honest mistake.

Dalia: Dalia Levin reporting from "Solomon's Day Court," where all Israel now stands in awe of the king's divine wisdom.

Advisor: That's a wrap.

SOLOMON BUILDS THE TEMPLE

I Kings 4:1-7:51

Narrator: Solomon's rule extended over all kingdoms from the Euphrates River to the land of the Philistines and the boundary of Egypt. Israel and Judah were as numerous as the sands of the sea.

Solomon: The time has come to build a House of the Lord. With the gifts of my friend King Hiram of Tyre and using the forced labor of the citizens, we are ready.

Secretary: It is just what God promised. And we've been taking bids from contractors.

Solomon: Cost is not important.

Secretary: In that case, I will expect a Rosh Hashanah bonus.

Solomon: Bring in the contractor.

Harry: Honor to be here, your majesty. I represent Harry's Builders of Hebron. Foundations are the base of our business. I'm Harry.

Solomon: I'd have never guessed. I need a time frame for the building of the foundation, the walls, and the basic house.

Harry: Let me pull out my abacus. Two reds plus a yellow . . . fifty years!

Solomon: Fifty years? You know, Harry, I've heard some talk about Harry's Builders using substandard straw in some of your bricks. A sudden government investigation could shut your business down, couldn't it?

Harry: Oops. That little red circle was on the wrong side. It will take seven years.

Solomon: And be sure to use only the best of materials. I'll be watching.

Harry: We'll use designer stones and lumber.

Secretary: Here's the interior designer.

Designer: Your majesty. It is such a pleasure.

Solomon: I want the inside of the Temple to look magnificent.

Designer: I would go with a jungle motif.

Solomon: I want a Temple, not a zoo.

Designer: Well, if we are going to be conservative, I suppose we could go with basic cedar wood.

Solomon: Hiram has sent me more than enough wood.

Designer: How insulting. I have my own suppliers. What else do you want?

Solomon: It's got to be a place that is special.

Designer: Yes, yes, I see it now. I'll give you an interior that oozes with inspiration.

Secretary: Oozes with inspiration?

Designer: It's designer talk. I see cherubs with an overlay of gold. As a matter of fact, I see gold everywhere . . . and purple and linen and silk. Ooh, ooh, what a vision I'm having. I'm in a creative frenzy! Servant, bring me a wine cooler, I have work to do.

Secretary: The craftsman who specializes in bronze is here to speak with you now.

Hiram: I am Hiram of Tyre. Yes, I have the same name as the king of Tyre. Yes, I live in Tyre. No, we are not related. Yes, I am an Israelite.

Secretary: That's amazing. You answered my questions before I asked them.

Hiram: It saves time. What job do you want me to do?

Solomon: Here's the list. But most importantly, I want you to create two elegant columns of bronze.

Hiram: That is going to take a long time to do.

Solomon: So let's begin.

Hiram: Hello, Mom. This is Hiram. No, not the king Hiram, your son Hiram. I'll be late for dinner. How late? Two years. Three years at the latest. Mom . . . hello . . . ? She hung up.

* * *

Secretary: The people from Feivel's Furnishings want to know where to put everything.

Fruma: We have a delivery of a table for bread, ten lampstands, some basins, snuffers, fire pans, and an altar of gold.

Solomon: Put the altar in . . .

Designer: Please, let me do my job. Bring those priceless items over here. Watch it with that altar. It is made of gold. You just can't find good help these days.

Solomon: It looks like things are almost done.

Designer: All that is left are the sacred donations of silver and gold from your father King David.

Solomon: The holy Temple is finally built. How did we ever do it?

Designer: You'll understand that better when my bill comes.

DEDICATION OF THE TEMPLE
I Kings 8:1-9:9

Secretary: Solomon, we have to go over the details for the dedication of the Temple. The time has come!

Solomon: Who's coming to this gathering?

Secretary: We invited all the elders, the tribal leaders, the ancestral chiefs, my in-laws, and a zillion dignitaries.

Solomon: Was there no way to cut down the guest list?

Secretary: You wanted the whole country invited. This is what we call a major party. I had to make my hair appointment three weeks ago. And forget the manicurist.

Protocol: Solomon, it's time to review the ceremony.

Solomon: I want it kept simple.

Protocol: We have the Priests and Levites carrying the Ark of the Lord up to the Temple while you and the people are making sacrifices. There will be more sheep and oxen than can be counted.

Solomon: What happened to simple?

Protocol: If you wanted simple, you should have hired Bubbles the Party Clown.

Secretary: Bubbles was out of town.

Protocol: This is the biggest thing to happen in years. Solomon, when the Ark is in the Temple and the two tablets are placed in the Holy of Holies, you will give a speech.

Solomon: Nobody told me about a speech.

Protocol: Talk about the promise God gave to David that you would build the Temple. Then give praises. Improvise!

Secretary: The shofar is blowing. That's our cue. Good luck, your majesty.

Solomon: Nobody told me about a speech.

Protocol: Everything is going so well.

Priest 1: Everybody start on your left foot. We don't want to drop the Ark.

Priest 2: There's no need to be so neurotic.

Priest 1: The last guy who touched the Ark was zapped by a blast of light when David was bringing it up to Jerusalem.

Priest 2: Which foot do we start on?

Priest 3: Bring it inside the Sanctuary so we can perform the ceremony.

Priest 2: The Ark is now in place. We can begin.

Priest 1: Look at the Sanctuary. It's beautiful. Look at all that gold!

Priest 3: I can't see anything.

Priest 2: The whole place is filling with a thick cloud.

Priest 1: I don't smell fire. The smoke detectors aren't going off. That means that this cloud represents the . . . uh, oh.

Priest 3: Do you think it is what I think it is?

Priest 2: Am I missing something here?

Priest 1: The presence of God has entered the Temple ... and I want my mommy!

Priest 2: This is awesome. Hey, where did everyone go? Um, I guess it's just me and the thick cloud. I don't think we're supposed to stay here any longer.

Protocol: Did you perform the service?

Priest 1: We couldn't do it. The cloud is too thick.

Protocol: Solomon, say something. Everyone is getting nervous.

Solomon: The spirit of God is with us in the Temple, and may it dwell here forever.

Secretary: Great opening. Keep going.

Solomon: God has fulfilled the promise made to my father. I have built a House for the God of Israel and in it I have set the Ark.

Protocol: I'm going to go check on the sacrifices. I hope there's enough food.

Secretary: We ordered 22,000 oxen and 120,000 sheep as sacrifices.

Protocol: That should make everyone happy.

Secretary: Everyone except the sheep.

Priest 1: Start the fires up. Solomon is almost finished.

Secretary: What did he say?

Priest 1: He warned us to stay on the path of God. He said that the Temple doesn't really contain God, that God's greatness extends throughout the universe. Then he asked that God hear the prayers of all of Israel and help and pardon us.

Secretary: Just hearing that makes me breathless.

Priest 2: Are you sure it's not the smoke from all the sacrifices?

Protocol: By my calculations, this party is going to last fourteen days.

Secretary: And it is truly magnificent. Much better than Bubbles the Party Clown.

Bubbles: Hi, I'm Bubbles. I just got the message. Where do I set up the balloons?

* * *

God: Solomon, I have heard the prayers that you offered at the consecration of My House.

Solomon: Did You like it? I thought it was a rather good speech.

God: Keep My commandments and your descendants will always be on the throne of Israel.

Solomon: I can live with that.

God: If you and your children turn away, I will sweep Israel off the land and reject the House that was consecrated to My name.

Solomon: I think we can all live with that.

THE QUEEN OF SHEBA
I Kings 9:15-10:29

Chairlady: Ladies, I hope you've all enjoyed your goat cheese finger sandwiches. Today's luncheon was prepared by our newest member, Mrs. Simcha Dimcha. Let's begin our meeting with a report from our social chairwoman, Yenta Telebenta.

Yenta: Ladies, we have competition. The whole city is talking about the Queen of Sheba. She came into Jerusalem today with a very large staff and with camels bearing spices, gold, and precious stones. You could kill for her wardrobe.

Member 2: Can we talk about the queen? She is gorgeous. You can tell that she doesn't do dishes or clean her own room. I've heard that she has come to Jerusalem because of Solomon's reputation for great wisdom.

Member 3: Be serious. Solomon owns half of the world and Sheba wants to be in on the action. She is one smart cookie. By the way, I heard from my sister's friend's cousin's aunt by marriage, who works at the palace, that Queen Sheba has dandruff.

All: No!

Yenta: According to my information, the queen has presented the king with some very difficult questions to test his wisdom.

Chairlady: Thank you, Yenta. By the way, if anybody has an extra ticket to the reception honoring Queen Sheba, I'll give you ten shekels for it.

Member 3: Are you kidding? You can scalp tickets for a hundred shekels. This is the social event of the decade.

Solomon: The answer to your fiftieth question is ten to the fourth power.

Sheba: Correct. You have answers for all my questions. You are as wise as they say you are.

Solomon: You're making me blush.

Sheba: You're cute when you blush. And your wealth matches your wisdom.

Solomon: What makes you say that?

Sheba: You're sitting on an ivory throne covered in gold.

Solomon: Iron is so cold.

Sheba: Your entire set of cups and utensils are golden.

Solomon: I like the color.

Sheba: You have 12,000 horses.

Solomon: It's a hobby. Some people collect stamps, I collect horses.

Sheba: You have made the Amorites and Hittites slaves, and you have your own people serving you as warriors and as officials.

Solomon: Good help is hard to find.

Narrator: Shortly afterward, the queen presented Solomon with gold and a vast shipment of spices. King Solomon, in return, gave the queen all that she wanted. Everybody agreed that the summit went well, and the queen returned to Sheba, a very happy woman.

Chairlady: Our final report this afternoon is from our athletic chairlady, Jodi Jockowitz.

Jodi: If you put your money on Balaam's Steed in the King Solomon Chariot races, the horse paid four on the shekel. The bookie should be here shortly, for those of you who want to place bets this week. According to my sources, Solomon is going to be exporting some of his finest horses to Aram for breeding purposes.

Member 2: It's going to prove interesting to see how that affects the horse world.

Jodi: Solomon's love for horses has created a bonanza for our club, ladies. Remember, ten percent of every bet placed goes into our club's checking account.

Member 4: I have an idea. Now, that King Solomon is building up his fleet of ships in the port of Ophir, we might be able to sponsor yacht races. That might be a real money maker.

Chairlady: Why should King Solomon be the only one taking in gold and silver? Ladies, we've got work to do. Meeting adjourned.

SOLOMON'S DECLINE
I Kings 11:1-43

Attendant: King Solomon, your wife is here to see you.

Wife: Solomon, we haven't talked in a long time.

Solomon: Didn't we speak yesterday?

Wife: That was Dalia.

Solomon: Which one are you?

Wife: I'm Sonya. You married me two years ago.

Solomon: That's right. You are a Moabite.

Wife: Actually, I'm an Ammonite.

Attendant: Sire, Sonya is number 892.

Solomon: How many do I have now?

Attendant: You currently have six hundred ninety-nine royal wives and three hundred handmaidens. That is a grand total of nine hundred ninety-nine.

Servant: The daughter of the Hittite king has arrived for her marriage to Solomon.

Attendant: An even one thousand.

Wife: Solomon, I know you are getting old, but surely you haven't forgotten your promise to build me a shrine so I can worship my god Molech.

Solomon: All right. Whatever you want, I'll do.

Servant: Sire, you are building shrines for all these foreign gods. God Almighty will be angry with your turning away.

Attendant: And some of your wives come from peoples that we have been warned to stay away from.

Servant: How can you handle one thousand wives?

Solomon: I have a simple rule. When I'm not with the one I love, I love the one I'm with. Maybe I should write a song about it.

Wife: Do I get a shrine for my foreign god?

Solomon: Of course, and please take my new wife with you.

Wife: Great, still another bed to put in the wives' dormitory.

God: Solomon, you have greatly disappointed me. I warned you to follow My ways or there would be consequences.

Solomon: You only warned me once. I forgot.

God: I warned you twice. You have married foreign women.

Solomon: Okay, I'll admit it. I may have been a little indulgent.

God: One thousand wives.

Solomon: A lot indulgent.

God: You have built shrines to other gods and are guilty of not keeping the commandments. I will tear away nearly all of your kingdom, except for one tribe. For the sake of David, this will happen after your lifetime.

* * *

Ahijah: Are you the one they call Jereboam?

Jereboam: Who wants to know? I don't talk to just anyone.

Ahijah: I am Ahijah the prophet and I have a message for you from God.

Jereboam: I think I have time for this message.

Ahijah: I am tearing my robe into twelve pieces and I am handing you ten. What thoughts does this provoke?

Jereboam: First, I think you ought to put some clothes on.

Ahijah: The ten pieces represent the ten tribes that God will tear away from Solomon's throne. Because of his sins, only one tribe will remain his. If you will follow God's ways, you shall be given the northern kingdom of Israel.

Jereboam: Well, this certainly changes my plans. I thought I would be going into Dad's sparkling wine business. But, tell me, why me?

Ahijah: You have proven yourself an excellent supervisor of Solomon's forced labor. And you come from the House of Israel.

Jereboam: I better turn in my resignation to Solomon. I have a rebellion to run.

Ahijah: Let's get going. Solomon will not like this.

Solomon: I want Jereboam dead. I could handle trouble in Edom or revolts in Zorah. But Jereboam is an Israelite. Bring him to me.

Servant: Jereboam has fled to Egypt.

Solomon: Being king is not all it's cracked up to be. Pass me the cake on that gold platter.

Servant: Life is rough.

Narrator: And Solomon reigned for forty years and died. He was buried in the city of David his father. And Rehoboam, his son, succeeded him as king.